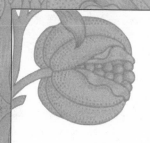

The
Magdalene
Mystique

Living the Spirituality
of Mary Today

Betty Conrad Adam

MOREHOUSE PUBLISHING

Harrisburg, Pennsylvania

Morehouse Publishing, P.O. Box 1321, Harrisburg, PA 17112
Morehouse Publishing, 445 Fifth Ave., New York, NY 10016
Morehouse Publishing is an imprint of Church Publishing Incorporated.

Cover design by Laurie Klein Westhafer

Page design by Carol Sawyer

Library of Congress Cataloging-in-Publication Data

Adam, Betty Conrad.
  The Magdalene mystique : living the spirituality of Mary today / by Betty Conrad Adam.
     p. cm.
  Includes bibliographical references.
  ISBN-13: 978-0-8192-2231-2 (pbk.)
  1. Mary Magdalene, Saint. 2. Gospel of Mary. I. Title.
  BS2485.A33 2006
  226'.092—dc22
                                                    2006024155

Printed in the United States of America

06 07 09 10 11 12   6 5 4 3 2 1

To my beloved husband Ken

Contents

Acknowledgments

Many people have created this book. How can I list a host of angels?

First, I want to mention my husband, Ken, to whom I dedicate this book. To Ken I give special thanks for our blessed life together and for his love, wisdom, and encouragement during the time I have been writing this book. I want to thank my sons, Mark and Michael, and my mother, father, brother who stand in the background of this book. To all my friends who were willing to read this manuscript in its early stages, I am deeply indebted. Their comments have added considerably to the value of its pages.

In my journey to the Magdalene, I have been inspired by the women and men of the Magdalene community. I have listened carefully to their insights in our study of the Gospel of Mary. We have struggled together to bring forth our thoughts about Magdalene spirituality. If it is true that gifts come in people as well as in packages, I can say that I have been gifted and graced.

I want to thank the dean of Christ Church Cathedral, Joe Reynolds, and my colleagues there and many friends for their support of the Magdalene community that emerged out of Brigid's Place. A celebration of Mary Magdalene on her Feast Day has become an annual event in that magnificent cathedral space. Also to the staff and directors and leaders of the interfaith Rothko Chapel, I give thanks. They have graciously provided their unique space for our weekly meditations and celebrations.

This book could not have been written without the work of the many scholars who have unearthed the Magdalene from lost history. The excellent work of Professor Jane Schaberg has been especially important in the evolution of my thought about the Magdalene and in the development of our community. Knowledge of Coptic and religious history provided by Karen King, Esther de Boer, and Jean-Yves Leloup has been crucial to the writing of this book as well as the translation by Marie-Luise Kalsi of articles written in German. To art historians Susan Haskins and those working on the recently discovered site at Dura-Europos, I am indebted, as well as to Susan Ashbrook Harvey, whose expertise in the Syriac tradition has added to the strength of these pages. To Jet Prendeville, librarian of the Art and Architectural Library at Rice University, I am also grateful. In general, I give thanks to ancient and modern writers in philosophy and religion whose work I have absorbed through the years. Their poetry and reasoning make up much of the background found in the book.

At Morehouse I am indebted to executive editor Nancy Fitzgerald, who first presented me with the idea of writing about our Magdalene community and has stood beside me in the preparation of this manuscript. I also want to thank my agent Susan Herner for her sound advice during the writing of this book. Without the technical expertise of many persons, the book could have not gone to press: to name a few, Ryan Masteller at Morehouse Publishing, Mona Rayachoti and Veronica Devoreaux at Christ Church Cathedral, and Candace Lynch who generously gave of her personal time and expertise in preparing this manuscript.

How can I thank a host of angels? I can't. I can only make a start.

Permissions

Permission has been granted to use three translations from the Coptic of the Gospel of Mary by Karen King, Esther de Boer, and Jean-Yves Leloup found in Appendix B. These translations have been brought together as a convenience to the reader interested in a thorough study of the alternative possibilities in language and content of the Gospel of Mary. The individual translations are found in the books of these specialists: Karen King's *The Gospel of Mary of Magdala*, Esther de Boer's *Mary Magdalene: Beyond the Myth* and *The Gospel of Mary*, and Jean-Yves Leloup's *The Gospel of Mary Magdalene*. Their generosity in allowing the combination of their translations to be used in this book is greatly appreciated.

I am grateful to the following individuals and institutions for granting permission for the use of visuals in this book: The Art Archive, Yale University Art Gallery, New Haven, Connecticut. Photographed *in situ*; Biblioteca Medicea-Laurenziana, Florence, Italy; The British Library, London, England; The Menil Collection, Houston, Texas; Antikenmuseum Basel und Sammlung Ludwig, Basel, Switzerland; *The Westminster Historical Atlas to the Bible* and permission granted by Westminster John Knox Press; Yahoo! map of Syria (permission sought).

1

Prologue

THE INSPIRATION FOR THIS BOOK is Mary Magdalene herself. It is also inspired by the women and men in a contemporary Magdalene community in Houston, Texas. We are fascinated by recent discoveries that have transformed her from a model of penitence into a spiritual leader. We're drawn to her, for we too, the people of God, are rising out of the dust of a theology that has stressed our sins at the expense of our shared humanity and divinity. We are a people on a spiritual quest to reclaim our true humanness.

In the history of the Christian tradition, long after the Magdalene lived, long after the community of the Gospel of Mary gathered together, false images of Mary Magdalene were swept into moral stories about the sacred and the profane. In the West her character was lost under the label "prostitute," and her experience was manipulated into a story about our need to repent and reform. These stories sidelined the spiritual power of the Magdalene and our spiritual power within.

But now it's time to discard these old ideas and to take up truer ones. In this book, we'll reflect on the "seeing" of the Magdalene and the visionary experience. We'll look at the process of breaking out of old stories about the Magdalene and other old stories. With new manuscripts in hand, we reject the false portrait that's been painted of her. We can re-imagine her and develop the embodied spirituality and the liturgies for celebration.

The Gospel of Mary's spirituality is a gift for our time. Today many men and women are on a spiritual journey. We're looking for God and searching. Some, in a kind of disillusionment or an estrangement from the traditional ways of seeing and feeling, are looking for the true and the real in every respect. Mary's lost Gospel tells us how a more deeply connected consciousness can happen to us all and how we can live in a greater sense of wholeness and shared peace. It's a Gospel that offers a seeing, feeling, and thinking spirituality.

Our community has begun to consider the soul damage inflicted on both men and women by an old way of thinking and feeling and its emphasis on "my group." We've recognized that we must begin the work of respecting all peoples. We must become shared peace.

It was only after I started writing this book that I began to realize the Magdalene story could help us move beyond our old way of thinking. The Magdalene had been disparaged and mislabeled out of ignorance or fear or politics. So it seemed to me that she represented any group that had been held in disrespect by those who wrote or spoke with authority. She represented any race or nationality or creed that had been stereotyped or demonized, any individual that didn't seem to belong. She represented the person who was different or strange.

I began to think that recognizing the Magdalene's story could move both men and women through a threshold into a more connected way of thinking and feeling. Surely her story is just one small piece in the history of human separations and oppositions, but it's made men and women who care about human relationships tune into its details, not only to learn about a biblical figure, but to learn about themselves and to seek change. It was a place to start.

In our contemporary community, we find that the more we study the Magdalene the more we choose to stay with her—to ask the questions, to re-imagine her within a broad historical and biblical context, to see from *within* a lost tradition how we might re-read the traditions we've learned, and to develop the spirituality of connection and peace.

Just as our Magdalene community is composed of both men and women, this book is written for both men and women. In *The Magdalene Mystique*, I invite you into our community, as we learn together who Mary Magdalene was, what kind of world she lived in, and what it means to envision our spirituality and our lives in new ways today.

2

Prelude

Rosamond

IT WAS AN OPENING. The phone rang and a familiar voice requested communion. I'd received any number of calls like this one. After all, I'd served as a pastor and priest in the Episcopal community for more than thirteen years and bringing communion to the sick is a regular responsibility—and one of the great joys of my ministry. But this call was different: the voice on the line carried the sense of urgency of someone battling an incurable disease, and it held a sense of the unexpected. The woman requesting Holy Communion attended the synagogue and retained her Jewish identity.

I'd acted as a pastor to Jewish friends before—I'd prayed with them and shared the Scriptures with them and counseled them in times of sorrow and joy. But never had I been called upon to act as a priest. But on this otherwise ordinary evening, Rosamond was calling on me, asking for communion, and placing me right in the middle of an ecclesiastical dilemma. For at least nineteen hundred years there had been a rule in the church that communion was reserved for baptized Christians. I'd never argued with the rule before, but tonight a friend with only a few months, or even weeks, to live, was asking me for the sacred bread and wine that was a remembrance of Christ's victory over death. I didn't ask about her beliefs, or if she had been baptized; it would have been absurd to do so under the circumstances. I simply said yes.

As I prepared my communion kit with the wine and the water and the wafers, I imagined the clock rolling back to the earliest communities, before baptismal rules were in place and before Judaism and Christianity were separated. Mary Magdalene came to mind, and as if following some long-ago instinct, I added anointing oil as well. I hadn't forgotten the baptismal rule and I wasn't flaunting it, but at that moment it seemed right to stand in the historical breach that had separated Judaism from Christianity for two millennia. The pastor in me took over the priest in me; compassion trumped canon law. I didn't look back, I didn't second-guess. With my kit in my bag, I got in the car and drove to Rosamond's house.

When I saw her in her white robe, her hair still wet from her bath, I couldn't help thinking of Thecla,[1] an early missionary with Paul who baptized *herself* in a vat of water when she was condemned to fight wild beasts. And my mind rolled even further back to the communities established even before Paul's—before the church had been transformed into a vast institution with rules and regulations like the one I was puzzling about that night. For some early communities, baptism was a washing away of the separations among people caused by race, gender, or class. I chanted to myself what may have been their baptismal words under my breath: "There is no longer Jew or Greek, there is no longer slave or free, there is no longer male or female" (Galatians 3:28).

Just for a moment I let my imagination take off. What if all the separations were erased: between nations and races, between Christians and non-Christians, between male and female, between those born into privilege and those into poverty and deprivation? What if all enslavements and unjust systems of domination had been banished all over the globe? What if the religious communities stood with the unjustly treated rather than for themselves? What if, seeking understanding, we finally opened our hearts with love to the truths of other religious traditions: the truths of the Hebrew Scriptures, the truths of the Qu'ran, the truths of native peoples, the truths of the Christian Scriptures both official and unofficial, and the truths of the sacred books and spiritualities of the East? What if all the religious traditions opened up to one another to bring peace to the world?

That night, as I offered the bread and the wine to Rosamond, all those breathtaking possibilities of divisions ceasing and peace coming into the world seemed real—all because Rosamond's heart and imagination had been touched by a first-century Jewish woman named Mary Magdalene, the intimate companion of Jesus.

As a child Rosamond had access through her rabbi to the Christian Scriptures, and she'd always been fascinated with Mary Magdalene. It was at a festival in honor of Mary Magdalene at our women's spirituality center in Houston that Rosamond had connected with our community. And now, as her own life was drawing to a close, the example of Mary Magdalene—who had persevered to the end and afterward—sustained and strengthened her. The Magdalene had witnessed the violent death of Jesus and been unafraid of confronting death herself. With the other women, she'd arisen early and gone to the burial site. And there, in that place of darkness, they'd received their blessing. Mary Magdalene was gifted to announce that she'd "seen the Lord." And there, for Rosamond, Mary Magdalene—Mary of Magdala, Mary, Mariam, namesake of Miriam the ancient Hebrew prophet—stepped into the rift between our religions. Identifying and belonging to one religious tradition, Rosamond felt connected to another through the strength and power of a woman's love and witness to prophetic words about the spiritual journey and life and death.

A Foot in Both Worlds

There, in the between, Rosamond felt perfectly at home. She imagined how easily Mary Magdalene—who would have been known as Mariam in her first-century world—had navigated both worlds. For

Rosamond, it was a source of strength, and a powerful means of connection, to think that another Miriam had followed the ancient Miriam, and that both were prophets in their own right. With tambourine in hand, the ancient Miriam had led the community in dance after the exodus victory through the Red Sea. And like her, Mary Magdalene led the other women to the tomb of Jesus. There she was blessed to see the risen Jesus and gifted with oracular speech—she became the first to announce to the brothers and sisters that she'd seen the Lord. That night, deep in conversation, Rosamond and I knew that both Miriams were honored in our traditions—at Passover and at Easter—and that the two Miriams and the other women with them formed a bridge between our religions.

Later centuries would devalue Mary Magdalene and transform her into something she was not. Miriam had suffered a similar fate when she challenged prophetic authority by saying, "Has the Lord spoken only through Moses?" But that night, Rosamond and I didn't talk about that. We wanted to think of the two Miriams as models of strength and courage. As we shared communion together, we shared the stories of these women and took comfort and strength from them.

Ancient and New

The story of Mary Magdalene is both ancient and new. Her Gospel of Mary was written in the early part of the second century but lost for centuries and only rediscovered in 1896. In it, there's no blame attributed to the Jews for Jesus' death. It stresses the connective teaching of Jesus, not his suffering and death. It instructs disciples to look within their hearts, not to authority figures in their search for the sacred. The Gospel of Mary proclaims the Magdalene's ancient apostolic Christianity, lost for nearly fifteen hundred years. But Rosamond and I found it again that night as though we'd been transported into an early Magdalene community. Fed by the bread and wine, nourished by our conversation, brought together by Mary of Magdala into a shared peace, we said our goodbyes. "We should never have been separated," Rosamond insisted as she stood at the door. But we were grateful that our rediscovery of Mary had brought us together.

3

❊

Finding an Ancestor to Bridge Separations

EVERY NOW AND THEN, people become aware of an ancestor they've long forgotten, and it changes their thinking in powerful ways. The ancestor's name catches on—who knows exactly why?— and an irrepressible energy coalesces around it. Something like this happened in the nineteenth century with St. Francis of Assisi. Francis had been revered in his lifetime in twelfth-century Italy and his popularity continued until well into the fourteenth century. But for the next five hundred years—during the Renaissance and the Enlightenment—interest in Francis fell into decline. It took the Romantic Age of the nineteenth century to reignite a popular fascination with his story—his care for animals and nature, his simplicity, and his "un-churchy" style. Today the blessing of animals on St. Francis Day is one of our most cherished celebrations and Francis himself is viewed as a mystic and prophet of the environmental movement.[2]

When the ancestor has left writings behind, people are hungry to know what they have to say. Francis's Peace Prayer contains some of the most familiar and best-loved words of our day: "Lord, make me an instrument of peace: where there is hatred let me sow love." His touching metaphors—"sister water" and "brother wind"—are more popular than ever, and people are fascinated by the community he formed in the Middle Ages. For contemporary people, Francis has stepped out of the past and become part of our culture, intriguing us with his charismatic personality and leading us to fresh insights and new ideas.

Rediscovering an ancestor we can relate to—and are eager to stand with—is a remarkable event. I know this for a fact, because a group of us within the church, together with a few who have given up on the church, have rediscovered an ancestor whose story had been misunderstood and all but forgotten. Her name is Mary Magdalene, and we have created a community around her.

Divisions and Separations

For centuries we've accepted our divisions from one another, identifying ourselves by race, nationality, color, gender, and creed, and collecting ourselves into groups that are the "same." But these groups often stir themselves into conflict and oppose one another and create wars and conflagration. Today hostilities across our globe and environmental changes threatening future generations challenge more than ever our nonchalant acceptance of separated sameness. Embracing oppositional thinking is no longer an option for the people of this earth.

Inspired by our ancestor Mary Magdalene, our community has become more conscious of divisional, and divisive, thinking and the preferential treatment of "my group." We've recognized our responsibility in changing the level of respect we hold out to all people. And in the process of our soul journeying, our praying and thinking, we have come to a new understanding of who we are and how we belong to this earth. We're feeling more deeply rooted in this earth and in the good and gracious God of creation. We're learning to make peace within ourselves, both as strangers to ourselves and as friends to ourselves. We are seeking to become the connected and shared peace.

And we're using oil from our own lamps to look inside, deep into ourselves, and finding there a force that connects rather than divides. We believe this is a divine force that gifts us to become the peace, the *shalom*, the harmony, to become truly human and filled with a desire for the well-being of all. The word *shalom* in Hebrew carries important connotations of wholeness and well-being. *Shalom* is more than a greeting. It is a stability and connectedness we want for ourselves and all others.

In our community we think of ourselves as "betwixt and between." That's where Mary Magdalene comes in. She confirms our intuitions about holy mysteries and sees the invisible in the visible. She stands in the gap between cultural and religious separations. She brings together the ancient and the new, the Semitic and the European.

In a world that hasn't yet learned to respect all peoples, the story of Mary Magdalene—identified as a prostitute in the West and sometimes fused with the Virgin Mary in the East—needs to be boldly proclaimed. In our community we seek to move beyond the opposites of prostitute and virgin, beyond false judgments and blame, and beyond divisions and hostile separations. We choose to stand in the between with Mary Magdalene and recognize and understand ourselves as truly human, turning to Mary as an example of all that means.

The Garden Encounter

The moment we associate most profoundly with the Magdalene is her garden encounter with Jesus after his resurrection. The Gospel of John offers a tantalizing trace of that encounter—it's a meeting of hearts, a moment that enters the soul and doesn't let go. It's a resurrection moment for Jesus, the Magdalene, and for all. The moment of seeing changes the Magdalene's thinking and feeling. She is raised to a new level of living and created anew. Jesus sees her in the fullness of herself, calls her forth into the power of God within her, and empowers her over a threshold that's been holding her back. She is elevated by his words and can say, "I have seen the Lord" (John 20:18).

The Gospel of John only gives us a passing glimpse of Mary Magdalene. But happily for us, there's a fuller account of our ancestor's story in another book—the Gospel that goes by her name.

The Gospel of Mary Magdalene

Written in the early part of the second century in the framework of an ancient world, the Gospel of Mary Magdalene is a Gospel of our deepest roots, filled with fresh insights for us today. It offers a Jesus who teaches that nature is good and that our true nature is rooted in the Good, a Jesus who greets his disciples with his peace and boldly instructs his disciples to "acquire my peace within yourselves."[3] It's this teaching to turn inward into peace that is so remarkable. It's a call to come home to our shared humanity and divinity. Grounded in our original Good, we can develop the peace by starting with ourselves. All of this is within our reach. We can become whole in soul, body, mind, and spirit. We may choose to do this. This peace begins within and spreads out into harmonious relationships and to connections beyond our ordinary ones. Moving from the inside out, we can become the shared peace.

Mary Magdalene understands this teaching of Jesus, as does Levi, who may be the tax-collector in the Gospels of Mark and Luke. We know that in the first-century culture a tax-collector was despised and excluded. Interestingly, in the Gospel of Mary, it is a tax-collector and a woman who first grasp the teachings of Jesus and can interpret the teachings to the other disciples. Levi says, near the close of the Gospel: "We should clothe ourselves with the perfect Human, acquire it for ourselves as he commanded us, and announce the good news."[4] Levi speaks as though he's experiencing a process of becoming truly human that brings peace within him. Conscious of a divine force within that unifies rather than divides, he goes out to teach and preach.

In the Gospel of Mary, we catch a glimpse of what true humanness and peace might mean to us. Jesus, the Blessed One, offers his disciples his blessings of peace—not a set of beliefs to adopt in his name. His teachings become openings that lead us through a threshold into a deeper connectedness. The Gospel is a door, as is the mystery-laden Magdalene.

Till We Have Faces

C. S. Lewis in his masterful book *Till We Have Faces*[5] retells an old Roman mythological tale about Psyche and Eros. The breathtakingly beautiful Psyche is born the daughter of a king. She is not high and mighty but as natural as can be. Her beauty and goodness are so profound that it hardly strikes you when you're around her, for her beauty spreads out to whomever or whatever comes near, whether it's the mud, the rain, or a toad. It's only after you've left her that you are astonished at her beauty and quickness and tender care. Psyche's Greek teacher of wisdom used to say that Psyche was "according to Nature"—exactly what everyone and everything is meant to be.

In Lewis's reinvention of the tale, Psyche represents the human soul—you and me, innocent and confounded but always seeking our destiny. Psyche has not yet fully developed. She is the human soul in need of more experience. Through the gifts of nature and the gods, she moves more deeply into her own heart to find her way.

One gift that Psyche has becomes a great problem that breaks out in her relationship with her sister Orual. Psyche, it seems, has vision that is disastrously misunderstood and becomes the source of lethal jealousy and cravings. Psyche can "see" what her sister Orual and her Greek teacher, the Fox (who represent the voice of rationalism in their culture), cannot see. Psyche calls her sister to cross over into her "soul-house" and "fair dwelling place" to live within her vision. She cries out: "This is it, Orual! It is here. You are standing on the stairs of the great gate."

In much the same way, the Gospel of Mary—and the Magdalene herself—seem to be calling us, too.

4

Rediscovering Mary Magdalene

SOMEHOW I MISSED MARY MAGDALENE when I was a child in Sunday School, and even after I'd grown up. The vague words associated with her—exorcised demons and prostitution—failed to draw me to her. No interest or curiosity sneaked by my firmly ensconced moral sensibilities and I passed her by as a stranger, like some of the nameless women in the Bible—the woman at the well with five husbands, for instance, or the woman taken in adultery. As far as I could tell, Mary Magdalene was a background character in the New Testament who didn't have anything to do with me—and very little to do with the church.

I always liked Paul. My spirit had always been captivated by the visionary experiences and the can-do power of Paul the apostle. He was a man in his own right, taking charge in the way he saw fit. I dreamed of missionary work like Paul's in far-off places, could trace his journeys from Greece to Rome, and memorized his command to "put on the whole armor of God, so that you may be able to stand against the wiles of the devil" (Ephesians 6:11). I'd never made the connection between Paul's dramatic experience on the road to Damascus and the country of Syria. I knew nothing of Syria in the early days of Christianity, nor had I thought of connecting his visionary experience of "a light from heaven" (Acts 9:3) to Mary Magdalene. Visionary experiences of the Magdalene? I didn't know she had any.

That Mary Magdalene had founded communities as Paul had, or that communities developed under her inspiration or memory, would have never occurred to me. I knew the old story of the beginnings of Christianity—the one outlined by Luke—and according to that story, women weren't on the leadership team. In truth, I wouldn't have been ready for such claims and would have questioned the idea of women's leadership in the church. I'd always wanted to be part of the ministry of the church but imagined myself teaching Sunday School, or leading a women's Bible class, or even becoming a minister's wife. It never occurred to me that I'd become an Episcopal priest. And even after I was ordained, it would be years before I began to see Mary Magdalene as the beloved companion of Jesus and as a complex figure of visionary leadership, spiritual maturity, and strength, who understood the teachings of Jesus and could convey them to all of us.

An Awakening

I well remember the beginning of my awakening to Mary Magdalene. In the early 1990s a bright and well-read parishioner told me with excitement that Mary Magdalene was an apostle. With all the confidence of my seminary training, I quickly responded, "Oh, no, Edie, she wasn't one of the twelve apostles." Edie told me to read Susan Haskins' book on Mary Magdalene, so I did.[6]

And I was enthralled. It was as though someone had switched on a light. I dove into the scholarly literature that unravels, piece by piece, the bizarre and unconscionable alteration of the identity of Mary Magdalene—morphing her from a leader in the early communities, gifted with the blessing of Jesus, into a model of penitence for sexual sins. Some early church leaders recognized her apostleship and named her "the apostle to the apostles." But beginning in the fourth century her story was undergoing its radical change, and by the sixth century she was identified by church culture as the "woman from the city" in Luke's Gospel. Her story as the biblical model of reformed sexuality was then set in stone and later generations would only amplify it.

As I read Haskins' book, I began to think about the ways old stories and legends inform the spiritualities of the people of God, even if they're pure fiction. Some "old stories" revered in the church, I learned, aren't true at all, but fabrications created to manipulate and control. These so-called old stories, it seems, simply aren't old enough to be historically true.

And much later, when I was writing this book, I realized that I myself had switched on that light—with the help of grace and the Magdalene scholars. I had wanted to see the truth for myself. I wouldn't be left in the dark about the leadership of the Magdalene, her apostleship, and her ministry. What was at stake was the leadership, not only of women, but of other groups or races or nationalities that had been disparaged or thought not to belong.

What unconscious forces were at work here I can only speculate, but there was a certain force within me that began to lead me on to continue in this adventure. At some point in my investigation, an image of the beautiful Psyche, with a flaming lamp in her hand, moving into the darkness to discover the face of love, popped into my head—as though there were some connection. She seemed to be the perfect image for the scholars, with their well-oiled lamps, who had moved into the darkness to unearth the Magdalene. Perhaps they could, like Psyche, bring beauty back from the underworld to the human world.

The innocent ingénue Psyche[7] had shown up in the world and gone with the flow. Her destiny is meted out by those around her, especially the power structures that control her. The priest and king of the kingdom decide that it is *she* who must be sacrificed to the gods to relieve the land of its drought and famine and plague. And even when Psyche had been rescued from death by Eros, her god of love, she is forbidden to see. Yet there came a time when she needed to see. That time had come for me.

With Psyche's lamp somehow given to me, I began to realize that my rediscovery of Mary Magdalene was not just of interest to me, or to the scholars of religious history, but was a remarkable journey of discovery of mythic and universal proportions. Just as Psyche represented in myth the human soul making its way to enlightenment and truth, so this journey to the Magdalene was a soul journey for all of us and part of a general awakening.

I continued to sort through the various stages of the Magdalene's transformation. The more I read, the deeper I found myself in church history. I read portions of commentaries and homilies from the church fathers about women and Mary Magdalene that were hard to take—portions from revered annals that were filled with spite toward women and "the others" who were not "the same." And I knew in my heart of hearts that this afflicted mentality of accepting cultural divisions and separating out and excluding those that were different in gender or in some other way was not locked up in the distant past but still operating—perhaps unconsciously, perhaps not—in the culture and in the church today.

Traditional Gospel Stories

I learned how important it is to place these church commentaries in their historical context, looking at the issues that engaged people when sacred Scriptures were written. I learned to think of our sacred literature as a tapestry of various threads woven together at different times under different conditions. Some threads are barely visible in the depicting of biblical figures, while others are thick and wide and clamor for our attention. It seemed to me that one thread of tradition—very ancient, yet barely visible—was cherishing the experiences of Mary Magdalene. I began to run my finger across the tapestry of our history and tradition, looking for the slightest trace of the thread of the Magdalene and her ministry.

I wasn't surprised that the thread was hard to find. Ministries of women have never been much in the press, unless trouble surfaces, so it was reasonable to assume that the ministry of Mary Magdalene and the other women would likewise have received little notice. I began to understand how little interest had been taken in the Bible in individuating the women in the passion and resurrection narratives. The women who were present at the crucifixion were not at all clear in the memory of some of the Gospel writers and were treated as a group of outsiders. With few marks of individuality, their names were jumbled and variously forgotten. Perhaps they were inserted into the Gospel stories out of historical necessity or because they filled out the scenery and helped move the action along.

There certainly isn't much about Mary Magdalene in the official Christian Scriptures known as the "canon." Though she's mentioned in all four Gospels, it's only as a stitch here and there. Even the Gospel of John, which gives Mary speech, drops the thread of her story. There's no account of her call to discipleship and ministry or mention of her as a disciple or a prophet, visionary, or apostle. Paul doesn't even count her among those receiving resurrection appearances from Jesus:

> He appeared to Cephas, then to the twelve. Then he appeared to more than five hundred brothers and sisters at one time, most of whom are still alive, though some have died. Then he appeared to James, then to all the apostles. Last of all, as to one untimely born, he appeared also to me. For I am the least of the apostles, unfit to be called an apostle, because I persecuted the church of God. But by the grace of God I am what I am, and his grace toward me has not been in vain. On the contrary, I worked harder than any of them—though it was not I, but the grace of God that is with me. Whether it was I or they, so we proclaim and so you have come to believe (1 Corinthians 15:5–11).

I began to see how the biblical Gospels vary in their portraits of women. Some draw a patriarchal view of women, while others trace a more authentic face. Luke, for example, shows us "diminished" women who are "prayerful, quiet, grateful and supportive of male leadership."[8] In his Gospel, the active seeing of the women at the tomb is not emphasized as it is in the other Gospels (Luke 24:1–12). Rather it is what the women "found" (a subtle distinction) that is remarkable. The two angels in "dazzling" clothes do not give them a commission but ask them to "remember" (also a subtle distinction) the words of Jesus "that the Son of Man must be handed over to sinners, and be crucified, and on the third day rise again." Then the women are said to have told "the eleven and all the rest," but their words are received as "idle talk." It takes Peter—who gets up and runs to the tomb—to verify their account.

In Mark, however, the seeing of the women is stressed. Mary Magdalene and Mary the mother of James and Salome see that the stone has been rolled away. As they enter the tomb, they see an angel in a white robe. The angel gives them a commission, saying: "[G]o and tell his disciples, including Peter, he is going ahead of you to Galilee. There you will see him, as he told you." But the women are said to flee the tomb in terror and amazement, saying nothing to anyone. And the overall impression of the women in this original ending of the Gospel is that they are silent, terrified, and inadequate to the task of their commissioning by the angel (Mark 16:1–8).[9]

In Matthew, the women are given a vision of angels and the risen Jesus, who commissions them into action, saying, "Go tell my brothers to go to Galilee, and *they* [my italics] will see me there." (Here is a slight shift from Mark where the women are told, "There *you* [my italics] will see him.") The women in this Gospel carry out the commission, but their story, interrupted by the story of the guards, is dropped.

The Gospel of John differs, some scholars say, from Matthew, Mark, and Luke. One Magdalene scholar, Esther de Boer, finds in John that the women, though portrayed in domestic roles, are given speaking roles and a share in mission.[10] In John (20:1–18), the Magdalene is alone at the tomb and sees that the stone has been rolled away. Though her story is interrupted by the story of Peter and the beloved disciple, who race to the tomb to see first (verses 2–9), her story picks up again when she looks into the tomb and both sees and converses with the angels. Then she sees Jesus, who gives her a significant revelation and proclamation. She carries out the commission, saying that she has "seen the Lord." But the Gospel's final chapter—probably added later—doesn't include her experience in its list of resurrection events, ignoring the significance of her vision and teaching.

Seeing beyond the Gospel Stories

But when I looked beyond the Bible into other Christian literature,[11] I was astonished to discover her apostolic ministry stitched in threads that were thick and glossy. She is portrayed as a visionary and spiritual guide, asking questions and conversing with the other apostles as though she were a person in her own right.

In the Gospel of Mary, probably written in the early second century in either Syria, Asia Minor, or Egypt, Mary Magdalene plays a central role as an apostle of visionary and mystical experience after Jesus' departure. She is a "prophetic revealer to the other disciples"[12] and the Savior counts her "worthy." She assures the other disciples—Peter, Andrew, and Levi—that they have been prepared as human beings and need not be afraid. She is a reconciling presence in the face of conflict and disparagement.

In the Gospel of Philip, thought to have been written in Syria in the second century, she is said to be Jesus' companion: "Three women always walked with the master: Mary his mother, [her] sister, and Mary Magdalene, who is called his companion. For 'Mary' is the name of his sister, his mother, and his companion." (Two words are used in the text for "companion," the first of Greek origin and second of Egyptian origin having several translations: companion, partner, or consort, which adds to its multiple meaning.)

The Gospel of Thomas, probably written as early as the first century in Syria, also presents the Magdalene in dialogue with Jesus. It is in this Gospel that Jesus says "I am the light" and describes the Kingdom of God as "already spread out upon the earth" and "within you and it is outside of you" (Gospel of Thomas, sayings, 77a, 113, 3a). Thomas, however, takes on a harsher tone: at the close of the Gospel, probably added at a later date, Simon Peter says to the disciples: "Mary should leave us, for females are not worthy of life." When I read those words that seared into my mind and soul, I thought of all the harsh words groups have used to describe other groups that were not the same and continue to use in these so-called enlightened times of our unending saga of harm to one another.

Peter's words, however, are more an exception than a rule in the extrabiblical literature. In the *Pistis Sophia*, for example, an extra-canonical text probably written in Egypt as late as the third century, Jesus commends the Magdalene and encourages her in speech: "Blessed Mary, you whom I shall complete with all the mysteries on high, speak openly, for you are the one whose heart is set on heaven's kingdom more than all your brothers." Here was a Greek word, *parresia*, I had meditated upon before. It may be translated "openly" or "boldly," as in our Bible when Paul is said to be speaking boldly in Damascus after he had seen the risen Lord (Acts 9:27–28). And here in this extrabiblical text, Jesus is calling the Magdalene to speak similarly. Not only does the Greek carry the sense of "bold-ness" but also "courage," "confidence," "joyfulness," and "fearless-ness." These traits emerge as a gift of the Spirit for public ministry.

What was it about Egypt and Syria that seemed to foster these appreciative memories of the Magdalene? Were these flashes of the human desire to reconnect itself to all of nature, to the Great Mother, to the womb of the earth, to the voice of creation? In ancient Mesopotamia, in Sumer and the fertile Tigris-Euphrates river valley, and in Egypt, reverence for that fruitful divine voice had prevailed for thousands of years. What if that voice of creation was our voice, too, mostly suppressed until our time?

Here in these extracanonical texts was a trace of the Magdalene different from the biblical memory. It is clear from these texts that *some* followers of Jesus had remembered the visionary and apostolic Magdalene and that memory had been sustained for three or four centuries. One community had written the good news as they understood it in her name, presenting her as a person in her own right, model of strength and wisdom and a source of spiritual guidance. Why weren't those stories included in the Bible? Was it because Mary's ministry hadn't been noticed, or was it because it had received too much notice? Had her fuller stories been cut out of the developing tradition—and if so, why?

Mary Magdalene as an Apostle

Recent scholars have delved into those questions, producing abundant research in Magdalene studies. They've pointed out, for example, that the word *apostle* as used in the early days didn't refer exclusively to the twelve disciples of Jesus, though Luke used it that way in his story of the early church. By the time Luke was writing his Gospel and Acts, church structures and male hierarchy were firmly entrenched and the term *apostle* was no longer gender inclusive.

But for Paul, writing much earlier than Luke, the word apostle had a broader meaning. To him, the visionary experience—seeing the risen Christ on the road to Damascus—was the moment he was commissioned as an apostle, even though he hadn't been one of the twelve. He also refers in Romans 16:7 to a woman named Junia as an apostle, though her name was changed in later manuscripts to Junius, giving the impression that she was a man. Knowing that Paul used the word *apostle* to refer to himself because of his visions—and to the woman named Junia—helps us understand how we may say that Mary Magdalene is a visionary and an apostle too.

Knowing this helps us think about Mary Magdalene—and her experience at the empty tomb on Easter morning—very differently from the way we thought of her in early Sunday School. In the Gospel of John, she's the first to encounter the risen Jesus, who tells her to "go to my brothers and say to them, 'I am ascending to my Father and your Father, to my God and your God'" (John 20:17). Then John continues: "Mary Magdalene went and announced to the disciples, 'I have seen the Lord'; and she told them that he had said these things to her." Like Paul's encounter with the risen Christ on the road to Damascus, some early Christians understood Mary's encounter as an apostolic seeing too. The second-century Bishop Hippolytus of Rome gave Mary Magdalene the title "the apostle to the apostles."

To some early communities, Mary Magdalene was a visionary and an apostle, though over the centuries a much different picture came into focus. Sadly, it's not uncommon for families to rearrange the truth about relatives they're uncomfortable with or fear or find strange—and the Christian family isn't much different. Some families even engage in revisionist history, and just plain distort the truth.

So it was that Mary Magdalene morphed from honored apostle to penitent prostitute—an old story we now realize isn't old enough to be historically true. It was a creation of a false image that transformed her character. It's an ancient strategy that relegates to the margins those we fear because they're different from ourselves or have something we desire.

But today we're rejecting these old stories and seeing Mary Magdalene in a new way. There's a spiritual energy being created by her new image, a stirring and a mystique that's calling us to notice her, and this spark is telling us as much about ourselves, our past and our future, as it does about the Magdalene. We're breaking out of old stories, moving beyond formerly set boundaries and defining images, and evolving into something new.

I include for your meditation, this Hellenistic (323 B.C.E.–31 C.E.) funereal stele from Asia Minor, depicting two figures in front of the door of the tomb, one representing Death and the other, Woman. Below the two figures, on the left, is winged Psyche, and on the right is Gaia (Greek and Roman earth goddess). Psyche, with her arms enveloped in her coat, stands in a posture of grief for the bereaved. (Antikenmuseum Basel und Sammlung Ludwig, Basel, Switzerland. Photographed by Dieter Widmer.)

5

Zari

MY FRIEND ZARI AND I had a connection that neither of us could logically figure out, for our worlds had begun in distant places. Zari was of Persian ancestry and originally from Iran, and I was a native Houstonian with an indeterminate ancestry—perhaps German or Nordic or English or French. Who knew, except that it was European and that I was an American. Zari had moved to our city some years before with her family. She was always radiant, with long dark brown hair and brown eyes that danced in their welcome. She was devoted to Islam, and she and her family had found a small Sufi community near their home.

When she called me one afternoon from out of the blue, I was surprised. She came right to the point. Would I meet her to hear the Sufi teacher? Without any hesitation, I said yes. I'd visited a mosque before with a class that was studying Islam, but this was different. It wasn't a token visit. It was one woman connecting with another, as natural and spontaneous a gesture as anything could be. The fact that our religions were different wasn't important—it was about two friends sharing an experience.

As I made my way to meet Zari, feeling called to prayer, I remembered how moved I'd been when I had heard Muslims being called to prayer. My husband Ken and I were visiting the mostly Muslim island of Java in South Asia, walking toward one of the great wonders of the world—not a mosque but the largest Buddhist sanctuary ever built, Borobudur. As we approached the path to begin our ascent to the calm and peaceful faces of the stone-carved Buddhas, we heard a voice in the distance calling Muslims to prayer. The voice didn't feel competitive, and its tone was transcendent, opening up a space in the between. However spiritual the ascent at Borobudur was for us that day, it was the conjoining of Buddhism and Islam in one setting that I remember the most.

Tonight, my visit to the Sufi meeting house in Houston was profound, as I half-suspected it would be. I was welcomed and given earphones that would translate the teacher's message into English as he spoke. I'd remembered to bring a scarf to cover my head but hadn't known to wear white. As we entered the worship space, I saw the men on the right and the women on the left, all on their knees in prayer and reading, all dressed in white. Zari and I dropped down on our knees to pray alongside the other women. I picked up the Qu'ran and held it in my hands as the speaker began to teach. Tears welled-up from inside of me and poured down my cheeks—for all the violence and heartbreak over religion in the history of the world, for all the misunderstanding and false stories, for all the hatred and insistence that one side was right. I wept, for here I was on the floor with a people in prayer in the manner they were accustomed to. And though it wasn't my custom, I was in prayer with them and we were together.

The teacher spoke about a journey into self-knowledge, about the spirit that flows through us with a power to heal and transform us mentally and physically and spiritually. He spoke of our inner resources in the heart as a treasure of gold and silver hidden within us. Excavate that goodness, he said, so we may have unity, calmness and peace.[13]

As the teacher continued, I knew I was in familiar territory. It was the path inward to peace that the Gospel of Mary had been talking about, and the path of ascent at Borobudur that Siddharta Gautama in India had proclaimed. It was the chariot ascent of ancient mystical Judaism that Jane Schaberg[14] had found in the encounter between Jesus and Mary Magdalene in the Gospel of John. And here in this Islamic Sufi setting I was listening to a teacher who had also experienced the inward path. This path was what we in our small Magdalene community had found together in our study, a healing and transformative way into self-knowledge where we experienced joy and peace. This was what Zari had wanted to share with me. She, too, was becoming the peace.

Afterward, when we were outside, I told Zari about our Magdalene community, how we were seeking conversation with other spiritualities and religious traditions in our desire to become the shared peace. Then I told her about my new interest in Persian Christianity and launched into a description of an ancient Christian site in Syria that houses what may be the oldest image we have of Mary Magdalene and the women at the tomb of Jesus. The women are dressed in white, I was delighted to say, and their faces are carefully drawn in—as though they are thought of as individuals with actions of significance. They are visionaries and strong heroic figures in the process of an awakening and being born into something new. A spark of interest registered in Zari's eyes and we hoped to talk more about religion in Persia. We said our goodbyes, but we left with a sense that we had grown closer, even though our worlds were apart.

Later I brought the teachings of this Sufi master to our contemporary Magdalene community and we included his words about peace in our interfaith service at the Rothko Chapel. The Sufi teacher Salaheddin Ali Nader Shah Angha brings together the teachings of Islam and the teachings of Jesus in speaking of the fundamental principle of *Erfan*, known in the West as Sufism:

> Unless a subject is completely known, its benefits and, ultimately, the necessity to make effective plans for its fulfillment, [it] will

never be implemented. With regard to peace then, if the most eloquent words and ideas are presented to the public solely through speeches, books and declarations, peace will not be known. These exercises only provoke their audiences to entertain an imaginary hope for peace, in a possible state of euphoria, with the promulgators most likely achieving acknowledgement and honor. But it will not be long before both audience and advocate become disillusioned. . . . The Holy Prophet Jesus (peace be unto him) has said in his teachings to his disciples: Peace I leave with you, my peace I give unto you; not as the world giveth, give I unto you (John 14:27). The essence of these words, which are among the fundamental teachings of *Erfan*, declare that the world does not have peace, and therefore cannot impart peace. The true meaning of peace refers to the inner freedom and spiritual elevation of every individual. Only by spreading the teaching of such principles may peace reign.[15]

In our community we want to know completely the meaning of peace and to feel the inner freedom and spiritual elevation within ourselves. Perhaps then we can impart the shared peace.

6

Images for a New Humanity in Dura-Europos

ON THE WEST BANK OF THE EUPHRATES RIVER in Syria, in an ancient Christian building, is an image of what is taken to be the oldest surviving image of Mary Magdalene and the women at the tomb. The image was found in 1929 in a frescoed building in a village called Dura-Europos. "Dura" means "fortress" in Semitic languages and "Europos" honors its Greek founding around 300 B.C.E. Dura-Europos is a contraction that brings together the Semitic and the European—it was named Dura at certain times in its history and Europos at other times.[16]

Dura-Europas in the Early Third Century

The building itself is our most primitive evidence for understanding concretely how early Christians came together in a meeting house. Excavators report that the building had been a house church, a typical

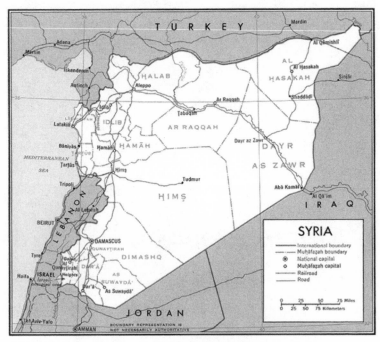

Map of Syria today. (Courtesy of Yahoo! maps. Permission sought.)

location for the followers of Jesus to convene after his death, but it had been converted into a building for worship that could accommodate as many as seventy persons. On the wall near the image of the women, located in the baptistery area, the year 232 is scratched—the presumed date of the building's construction. It was a time of persecution in the West under Roman emperors, eighty years *before* Christianity was legalized in the years 312–313 through an Edict of Toleration published by Constantine and Licinius, granting freedom of worship to a number of religions.

Though we mostly think of Christianity as moving westward toward Rome from its birth in Palestine, Christianity also spread to the east into other regions, and into Syria, where very early followers of Jesus established communities, and into what is now modern Iraq and Iran. It was on the road to Damascus in Syria that Paul experienced his vision of the risen Christ. In the first and second centuries, geographical regions came to be associated with certain of the twelve apostles: Syria was linked with Thomas and Egypt with Mark.

The Tigris and Euphrates river valley was a region that through history had fallen into the between—between Rome in the west and Persia in the east—both in the powers that dominated them and in the cultures and languages that influenced their thought forms. Dura-Europos had been variously conquered by the Persians and Romans—in 256 it was held by the Romans but was under siege from the Persians (Parthians). Before the attack the Christian building

Map of ancient Syria.

was intentionally buried to reinforce the city walls. After the attack and subsequent takeover by the Persians, the city was abandoned and the building remained buried until its recent rediscovery.

Dura-Europos is an important archaeological site. Its twentieth-century excavations have revealed an ancient city inhabited by peoples of diverse cultures of Greek, Roman, Jewish, Christian, Iranian, and Babylonian origins. A variety of artistic expressions within the city walls are still visible, and there is promise, as art historical research continues, they will reveal much about the historical context and values and convictions of these ancient peoples.

Adaptations and Overlap

At Dura we find artists making use of popular symbols and figures from their surrounding culture and adapting them to their own contexts.[17] Like other third-century Christian frescoes that have been recovered, the paintings at Dura show more overlap in their imagery and symbols with other religious traditions than Christian paintings show in later generations, when Christian identity had become more thoroughly defined. In these early years of the third century, as in Dura, we find more similarity and continuity with figures used previously in Greco-Roman religions than in future generations. Universal values of piety and prayer and virtuous living could be expressed using images and symbols that were not yet specifically Christian. It was a time of less separation between Christian imagery and Greco-Roman imagery. Christians could draw out their own Christian meanings in the adapted figures "without being overly self-conscious or apologetic for the borrowing."[18] It was a "graceful"[19] period of transition from pre-Christian symbols to Christian ones.

Jesus as the Good Shepherd

Religious historian Robin Jensen points to the figure of the shepherd carrying a ram on his shoulders above the baptismal font in the Christian building at Dura. This shepherd is an example of an adapted figure. The shepherd was a popular figure in Greco-Roman art as a symbol of humanitarian care. The image of Hermes, who as guardian of souls and guide to an underworld, may have been the Greek antecedent to the Christian imagery of Jesus as the Good Shepherd. The image of the shepherd would have been a particularly appropriate one for a baptismal setting that expressed rebirth. Also, there may have been an allusion to the Twenty-Third Psalm, in which the shepherd leads us beside still waters and anoints our heads with oil (the chrism used for anointing after baptism). But by the fifth century, in a more dogmatically oriented time, the figure of the Good Shepherd had almost disappeared, replaced in post-Constantinian times by more majestic figures of Christ as enthroned Lord.[20]

The paintings at Dura are early enough that to look for doctrine or dogma would be anachronistic. We can speak of doctrines and creeds only after the councils begin with Nicea in 325. Also, there is the issue of geographical location and isolation. Aphrahat, for example, writing in Persia a hundred years or more after the walls in the baptistery at Dura were painted, seems not to have known anything about the Council of Nicea, which was formally introduced into Persian Christianity in 410.[21]

There is some consensus among scholars that the painters who worked at Dura had an artistic vocabulary not derived from Rome.[22] If we look closely at the Gospel scenes depicted on the walls of the baptistery, we have the impression of an artistic tradition quite close to the Roman, but distinct.[23] In the painting of the women at the tomb we do not find what we have come to expect in the Greek East and the Roman West.[24] For me, there is a sense we are finding here in Mesopotamia a slightly different religious thought to which I am eager to connect. Linguistically and spiritually, the region is distinct from the Latin West and the Greek East. And there is similarity and overlap between religious expressions, and less separation, than will become the norm in later generations.

The paintings may have derived from the needs of the people rather than from the clergy and higher authority.[25] At Dura we may have a truly grassroots glimpse into the way the people of this time and this region understood Christian teachings.

Jewish Synagogue in Dura

In addition to the Christian house church that attests to a Christian community living in Dura, there is also a synagogue indicating the presence of a Jewish community. Interestingly, there are no creation stories represented on the walls of the synagogue, as we might expect, and the biblical scenes are interpreted through Iranian costumes and black and white Parthian (Persian) horsemen. Two art historians[26] note in the Dura paintings the influence of early Jewish mysticism, associated with Ezekiel and his experience in Babylonia, and there's been discussion about the mysticism that emerges from the synagogue art. Though the synagogue retains a clear Jewish identity, some of the decorations and ornaments derive from non-Judaic cultures— in one painting depicting the infant Moses, his sister Miriam, and Pharaoh's daughter, one art historian finds a Hellenistic understanding of Moses as human and divine, and the posture of Pharaoh's daughter suggests a reference to Anahita, a popular goddess in Iran associated by the Greeks with the Great Mother and Aphrodite.[27] Another has remarked on the ornamentation of nymphs and the beautiful Greek underworld goddess Persephone in the decoration of the synagogue.

Opposite: *Infancy of Moses with Miriam and Pharaoh's Daughter* (Dura-Europos synagogue). For our meditation, there are several actions depicted in this painting in the Dura synagogue. The figure on the far right is Jochebed, the mother of Moses. She is placing the baby Moses in his ark to save him from the Pharaoh's orders that all Hebrew infants are to be killed. A midwife stands next to her. In the middle of the painting are three attendants to Pharaoh's daughter in procession to the water. They carry a pitcher, a fluted bowl, an ivory box, and a shell-like vessel. In the next action, the Egyptian princess, having seen the baby in the ark, has stepped into the water to save him. We see Miriam, Moses' older sister (second figure on the left), standing *between* the Egyptian princess and Moses' mother, who in this action stands on the far left. The young Miriam, gifted with the capacity to heal the situation, is approaching the princess, asking her to hand over the baby so she can return the baby to his mother, whom she declares to be a nurse. Miriam's insightful and compassionate action has brought the baby Moses full circle and out of harm's way. (Yale University Art Gallery, New Haven Connecticut. Photographed *in situ*.)

Greco-Roman and Persian Temples

We cannot read back into ancient times the kind of religious toleration that the Enlightenment helped us frame,[28] yet the very exis-
tence of a synagogue and a Christian building in what was otherwise
a Greco-Roman city with different cultural forces at work speaks of
a kind of openness between religions. One art historian has seen at
Dura a "genuine and open-minded interest in all manner of religious
belief, association, and practice, ranging all the way from philosoph-
ical mysticism to so-called science of astrology and giving particular
attention to the cults of the eastern Mediterranean."[29]

At Dura-Europos one major civic shrine is a temple to Artemis,
an earth goddess in early Greek religion and mythology and, in a
later phase, a virgin huntress. She was especially concerned with
women and wildlife and children. The temple is built along Persian
lines and Artemis is merged with her Persian equivalent, Nanaia.
Also in the temple is a figure celebrating Aphrodite, Greek goddess
of fertility, love, beauty, marriage, and family life.

One block east of the temple of Artemis is a temple in honor of
the Syrian goddess Atargatis, also identified with Aphrodite, and
more specifically revered as the goddess of fish and seafarers; she
legendarily gave rebirth to Jonah in his early Babylonian form. A
number of other temples have been uncovered, among them three
in honor of Zeus, the sky god and leader of Greek gods; one in honor
of Adonis, the Syrian life-death-rebirth deity brought into Greek
mythology; and one to Mithras, who was popular particularly with
the Roman soldiers who encountered the god in Persia. Perhaps in
an atmosphere of artistic expression, unapologetic about its adapta-
tions and assimilations, in a multicultural city accepting varieties of
religious experience and practice, where gods and goddesses were
imagined alongside biblical figures, and separations and divisions
were not clear and distinct, a celebration in the Christian building
of the women as visionaries and models of humanity was possible.
Perhaps it even seemed natural.

Christian Building in Dura

Women at the Tomb. The women are holding torches to see and unguent jars for anointing. A star is placed on the left and the right of the sarcophagus. (Yale University Art Gallery, New Haven, Connecticut. Photographed *in situ*.)

Wall paintings are located in a room thought to have been a baptistery for the initiates into the new faith. The paintings seem to relate resurrection motifs to the experience of the men and women undergoing baptism. As you can see from the reconstruction of the three walls (on page 36), much has been lost. On the right wall is an image of a woman wearing a star. She is drawing water from a well. This may be the Samaritan woman to whom Jesus speaks in the Gospel of John (John 4:7–42). In speaking to her, Jesus stands between two culturally defined boundaries, one between Samaritans and Jews, and the other between men and women. The woman in the painting may be drawing out the "living water" given to her by Jesus and to the initiates in their baptism.

Many interpreters suggest that the paintings on the middle and left walls refer to the biblical passages of the women at the empty tomb and their revelatory experiences. These paintings are usually entitled *Women at the Tomb.* Of the two actions, one scene takes place outside the tomb (the middle panel) and the other, inside (the left panel).

The two scenes in the Dura baptistery differ from all later treatments of the subject during Constantine's reign in the fourth

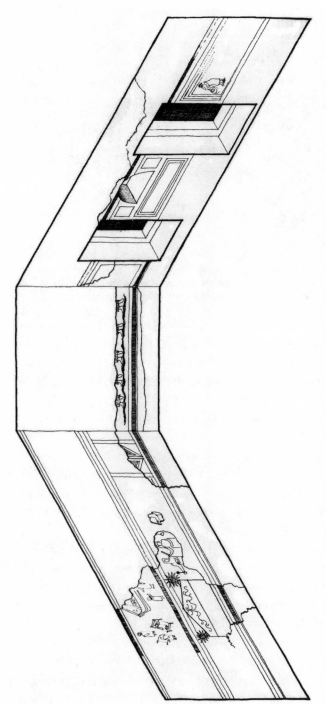

Reconstruction of three walls of baptistery (Dura-Europos Christian building). (Yale University Art Gallery, New Haven, Connecticut. Photographed *in situ*.)

century. The Dura painting, one expert says, stands "thoroughly alone."[30] In it, there are stars representing angels, which from a Syrian and Babylonian or Mesopotamian perspective isn't strange at all—there's evidence in both Jewish intertestament literature and in early Syriac writings, such as in Ephrem the Syrian, that angels were associated with astral powers. In the hymns of Ephrem, the angel of the Annunciation is identified with the star in the East that guided the wise men.[31] This inclusion of the stars may be a reference to Babylonian and Greek mystery religions.

Furthermore, there are no guards at the tomb and the women hold torches and unguent jars. In the Christian Greek orthodox tradition, the women carry incense burners. In the Roman West, neither incense burners nor jars are included in the artistic renderings. Typically in the Greek East two women, and in the Roman West, three women, encounter a seated angel outside the tomb. The sequel to the first encounter in the Greek East and in the Roman West is the scene in the garden, either with two women holding Christ's feet, as in the East, or the Magdalene in the "Don't cling to me" posture in the West.[32] In the Dura painting, the sequel to the first action of discovering that the tomb is open is the second action that takes place within the sepulcher itself.

And in the Dura painting there is a "dignity and solemnity of the figures and of the occasion, giving weight to that which by their presence they attest."[33] The figures are of heroic proportions, models of strength and vision—not cowering or weeping as in later Roman and Greek representations. Calm, impressive, and holy, the women move forthrightly to the tomb of Jesus. The powerful impact of the painting depends on the viewer's familiarity with the story of the women at the tomb—the rolled-back stone with visitations from angels and the anticipation of resurrection in this baptismal space.

In the first movement, the five move to the left, toward the slightly ajar door. All we have left of this action, a witness to the tomb having been opened and the stone rolled away, are the five sets of feet in procession, in boots of the Syriac fashion of the day, and the bottom frame of the barely open door. The tomb has been opened by the angel, who may in the original painting have been seated over the door. Alternatively, the angel may have been represented by a star.

The second movement occurs as we move to the left on the wall, following the first sequence. The women, coiffed and dressed in white festive garments and veils, have now entered the sepulcher where next they encounter angels.

The first woman, perhaps Mary Magdalene, holds a burning torch upright in her right hand, while the torch of the second female figure is held diagonally. Lit by the flames of their torches, the women move toward the sarcophagus against a red-purple background that represents the subterranean darkness. Each carries an unguent jar that identifies them as ointment bearers intent on anointing the body of Jesus, and for the initiates a sign of the chrism and the anointing of the Holy Spirit. As the viewer of this painting, we too await an epiphany and revelation.

I love the story of the excavators[34] as they first uncovered these panels. In the first stages of removing the earth, the stars were revealed, along with the tops of the heads of three figures. Some thought at first that they'd uncovered a painting of the wise men visiting the baby Jesus, guided by the star, as in Matthew 2:1–12. When more work of excavation had been done, the painting revealed the faces of women, carefully drawn in. To me, the initial intuition is apt—the painting is a representation of the wise women as models for humanity, visiting the tomb and anticipating a discovery.

Dr. Pasquale Accardo alludes to the possibility of a non-Christian antecedent, as well as a Jewish antecedent, for Mary Magdalene in the Dura painting. He speaks of the Dura representation of Mary Magdalene holding a torch in her right hand as a Psyche figure with her lamp "suddenly discovering again the true nature of her divine beloved." Accardo adds that as the Hebrew bride of the Song of Songs seeking her divine spouse and as the spiritual lover of Christ, she is a "major Psyche figure."[35]

A Space of Epiphany and Light

Scholar Gerasimos Pagoulator[36] gives his reading of the Dura paintings from within the context of three liturgical texts that were circulated in Syria in the second and third centuries. Chief among these texts is the Gospel of Philip. He interprets the painting as a liturgical procession depicting the women, as representations of both men and women initiates, before Christ's epiphany and after his entombment. The baptistry, this interpretation holds, is a space of epiphany and a manifestation of divinity. Its realistic sky in the room's ceiling, as well as the canopy over the vault of the baptismal font, represent the vault of heaven and the cosmic dimension in which the liturgical action takes place. The nature of Christ is light, and the participants, through baptism, are united to Christ and transformed into his likeness. "Christ is made present by the image of the Good Shepherd and united with the participants personally . . . the chapel is full of divine light, an element that characterizes also the divine nature of Christ."[37] In this interpretation, the liturgy is understood as appealing to the entire being of the individual initiates, who are transformed in intellect, senses, and emotions. The visual plays a major role in the communication of knowledge to the participants, who experience a resurrection as they are transformed in the present.[38]

Though Pagoulator does not go in this direction, it's possible to interpret the three figures in the interior tomb chamber as the three women mentioned in the Gospel of Philip who "always walked with the master: Mary his mother, [his] sister, and Mary Magdalene, who is called his companion." Mary Magdalene, from the perspective of the Gospel of Philip, is characterized as the one who can see the light. Like Jesus, her capacity to see the light is related to her capacity to love.

All this may sound strange to our twenty-first century ears, particularly to those brought up in the scientific and technological West. But it would be familiar to the Syriac Christians who authored the Gospel of Philip, and perhaps to the Christians at Dura. Their models for a new humanity about to be born would have been the Good Shepherd and those who, like the Good Shepherd, were connected to the mystical light.

Because of the quality of the work and the size of the figures, some experts think this painting was highly important within the context of the other paintings adorning the walls of this early house church. Whether or not the size of the figures as representations of humanity attests to the significance and leadership of actual women in the Dura community, we cannot know at this stage of research. But perhaps, in an open atmosphere of poetic sensibility and symbolic expression, it is not impossible to think that gender separation for leadership hadn't yet taken hold in the community, and that here we have traces of an egalitarian community whose baptismal room this is.

Ancient Dura-Europos in Syria is worthwhile for us to contemplate. It takes us back to a Greco-Roman environment that included buildings for both Christians and Jews. We know very little about the stream of early Christianity that flowed through Syria in the first and second centuries that would have found expression at Dura, but the idea that Syriac-speaking peoples would have developed a spirituality that differed from that of peoples speaking Latin and Greek is now receiving the scholarly attention it deserves. We forget that by the third century the Christian world consisted of three major cultural centers: (1) the Roman West, (2) the Greek East, and (3) the Syrian Orient. Dura is located on the frontier of the Syrian Orient, which moves across Iran into Persia, India, and China. Syrian spirituality, scholars suggest, may have differed from mainstream Greco-Latin spirituality in being rooted in an approach that gives rise to metaphors, parables, symbolic deeds, and visions. It's not based on an antithetical logic of Greek philosophy but more on assimilations and vision. It expresses itself in poetry, perhaps a carryover from the Semitic influence and the spirituality of Jewish Christianity.[39] In this atmosphere women were imaged as spiritual visionaries and models of strength and courage for a new humanity and as playing significant roles in the events of Christianity. Perhaps here in Dura-Europos we have a more authentic face of women in early Christianity than in the biblical narratives. Here the women are not outsiders but imaged as spiritual models for initiates into the community. Perhaps here we have a lost thread of Magdalene memory.[40]

It's important to consider that in Syria there may have been a stream of Christianity without an either/or logic but one that was symbolic and figurative and an expression of popular piety. The church never objected to this way of thinking and feeling—it was only much later, at the time of the creedal controversies in the fourth and fifth centuries, that Syriac Christianity became embroiled in controversy and lost its status in the flow of mainstream thought.

7

The Replacement of Mary Magdalene

HOWEVER MYTHICAL AND SYMBOLIC Mary Magdalene and the women were becoming to me as models of the human soul finding its awakening and enlightenment and rebirth, I wanted to discover who Mary Magdalene was as a person in her own right—who she was as a living, historical woman before her transformation by church leaders.

Who was she, as sorted out from the other women in the Bible, including those who were also named Mary? The task was complicated by the sheer number of Marys in the Bible! There's Mary the mother of Jesus, Mary of Bethany and sister of Lazarus, Mary of Clopos, Mary the mother of James and Joseph, and "the other Mary." Ambrose, a fourth-century Latin Father, admitted the problem of distinguishing the Marys and the confusion in the Bible about who was—and who wasn't—present at the life-changing events: "Were there Mary, the sister of Lazarus, and Mary Magdalene, or more people?"[41] This was the first problem: differentiating the Marys.

I soon discovered my desire to find the historical Magdalene would lead me back again into Syria. The Magdalene energies (that I had learned to call a "mystique," in the sense of a "mysterious attraction" and/or "veneration") that had taken me to Dura-Europos would lead me into commentaries of Christians living a hundred years or more after the painters at Dura, to places whose contemporary cultures I knew very little about. And these modern Muslim and Arabic-speaking nations (modern Turkey, Syria, Iraq, and Iran) were much in the public consciousness again, the setting of yet another war in the Middle East that seemed to have sprung up overnight, further engraining the kind of oppositional thinking I hoped the Magdalene would help erase.

Ancient peoples, of course, knew much about hostile conflicts and separations. Syria itself had tried to survive in the ongoing conflicts between Rome and Persia. Perhaps there were lessons in ancient writings that could assist us today. Also, it would be good to connect to the ancient peoples of these nations with the hope of finding channels to bridge separations today. I thought of Zari and her Persian ancestry and our intuitive connection and interest in the shared peace. And I thought of the Magdalene, as portrayed in the Gospel of Mary, as a reconciling presence in the midst of disparagement and conflict. I began to think of the early baptismal words as applicable today in their meaning: there is no longer American or Syrian or Iranian or Iraqi, no longer Christian or Muslim, no longer enslaved or free, no longer male or female. We are all one in the human race, seeking to be truly human. So I began to look to Syria to see what I could learn.

The Syrian Orient

In my sorting out of the various Marys from Mary Magdalene, Syria seemed a good place to start: the Syrian Orient. The term "Syrian Orient" refers to a huge region in the ancient world where Syriac was spoken and became the liturgical language for Christians. The regions corresponded to areas now found in Israel and Palestine, eastern Turkey, Lebanon, Syria, Iraq, Iran, and parts of India. Syriac is a dialect of Aramaic, itself a dialect of Hebrew. It developed out of a particular dialect of Aramaic spoken in the region of Edessa (modern Urfu, in southeast Turkey) over the course of the first century C.E. During the third century it spread as a language notably used by Christians.[42]

As we have seen, the Gospel of Philip, probably written in Syria in the second or third century, had carefully distinguished three Marys: "Mary his Mother," "his sister," and "Mary Magdalene, who is called his companion." It would be some time before I would pick up on the significance of the next sentence in the text: "For 'Mary' is the name of his sister, his mother, and his companion." It's a slow process to move from West to East, from a Western tongue to Syriac, and into thinking of "type."

Ephrem the Syrian

I also turned to the writings of Ephrem the Syrian, a poet and a musician as well as a theologian. Here was a refreshing voice. I could tell immediately I was in a mind-set and language that differed from my usual Western readings. Also, there was a sense of a contemporary relevance in his approach to Christianity. With my energies moving me on, I felt I might have a chance of breaking out of the old Eurocentric story of my early religious training as I learned more about Ephrem's—and ancient Syrian Christianity's— connections to nature, visions, and women.

Ephrem begins his thinking by asking a question, then offers a number of answers, some which go on for pages, with metaphors and poetic images that move us emotionally but suggest rather than assert. Readers are required to think and rethink for themselves and ask, "How does this apply to my life?" Ephrem's imagery felt to me more connected to nature, to the sun and to the stars, as though he himself were deeply connected. I began to think that perhaps I had found another saint, like Francis of Assisi, who was speaking for the environment. Ephrem also gave credence to the visionary experience and its mystical dimensions, reading the garden encounter in the Gospel of John as a profound experience for both

Jesus and "Mary." When Jesus says, "Do not hold on to me" (John 20:17), Ephrem interprets, he "pours forth abundantly, filling her with a new proclamation concerning his ascension."[43] The Oriental mind, I began to understand, formed itself in different ways from that of the Greco-Roman.

In Ephrem's commentary I found a connection to women, specifically to the birthing process to which the Christian rebirthing process is likened, with no shyness or embarrassment at mention of the womb. Female imagery runs through his pages of commentary on what was his Bible. Perhaps foundational to Ephrem's thinking was the ancient image for expressing the divine as the great womb or the cosmic egg out of which all elements emerge and in which human and nonhuman creatures live together.

Yet there were harsh tones in Ephrem, like the ones I had seen in the Gospel of Thomas: "How the serpent had killed the entire human race through Eve."[44] Also, there are harsh tones against the Jews, whose faith is said to have been surpassed by Christianity.

Still, I felt my venture into Syriac Christianity would be empowering. I had crossed over into the Syrian Orient, where the Holy Spirit in the earliest centuries was presented with feminine images rising out of the grammatical gender of the noun for spirit—*ruha'* is feminine in Syriac, as *ruah* in Hebrew—and out of the verbs that describe the Spirit's action. The Spirit was said to "hover" over the waters in the beginning of creation, like a mother bird hovering over the nest, and was connected to the dove at the baptism of Jesus. At baptism the Spirit was thought to descend from heaven and hover over the waters, and those who are baptized put "her" on.[45] This kind of imagery felt liberating and elevating. I could more easily identify myself as made in the image of and likeness of the Spirit of God with this imagery. Was this a trace of the human desire to remain connected to Mother Earth and the voice of creation?

The Magdalene in Syriac Writings

Yet in Ephrem there is far less about Mary Magdalene than there is about the Virgin Mary, and his characterization of the Magdalene began and stopped with the idea found only in Luke that she was a follower of Jesus from whom seven demons had come out (Luke 8:2–3). The number seven had captured Ephrem's attention and he likens her seven demons to those mentioned in the story in Matthew of an unclean spirit going out of a person (Matthew 12:43–45). It is noteworthy that the Magdalene's demons in Ephrem are not understood as sexual demons, as they would be years later in the Western branch of the church. In general, in the Eastern branch of the church, Mary Magdalene was never characterized as a sexual sinner as in the West.

The Name "Mary"

Though this part of Ephrem was jarring, by far the most discouraging aspect of Ephrem in my search for the historical Magdalene was his use of the name "Mary" in his commentary of the famous garden encounter described in the Gospel of John. By using the name "Mary," he links the Magdalene's action in the garden to those actions we associate with Mary the Mother of Jesus, at the birth (Matthew 1:18–25; Luke 2:1–7), at the wedding at Cana (John 2:1–12), and at the cross with the beloved disciple (John 19:26–27). The result of the naming is that Mary Magdalene is dropped out of the story of the resurrection. So the story of the Magdalene in John's Gospel is transformed into a story about Mary the Mother.[46] It is Mary the Mother who does not recognize Jesus outside the tomb, it is Mary the Mother who is said to confuse him with the gardener, it is Mary the Mother to whom Jesus says "Don't touch me," when she expresses affection for him "like a mother."[47] It is Mary the Mother who, according to Ephrem, receives the vision and the apostolic commissioning in the garden and is said to stand for the Second Eve.

The Replacement of Mary Magdalene by the Virgin Mary

For the most part in the Syriac tradition, the treasure of the Magdalene story—her first witness to the resurrection and her commissioning—was given over to Mary the Mother of Jesus. It may have been for the sake of finding a symbol or a type, a Mary who could stand for the new Eve and the Church, or for explaining why the risen Jesus first appeared to a woman rather than to a man, a question that Ephrem brings up in his commentary. He answers his own question by noting the presence of the one whose name was "Mary" at the tomb and at the birth, and the recompense "she who bore that name" accomplished. Connecting the birth narrative and the tomb narrative is important to Ephrem.

Perhaps the replacement of the Magdalene by the Virgin arose out of an overriding devotion to the Virgin Mary that had already developed in Syria, or was connected to the discipline of virginity, for both men and women, which developed very early in Syriac Christianity. This early tradition encouraged a life of celibacy, or chastity within marriage (restricting sexual activity so that there are only one or two children). This attitude was part of a very strong eschatological expectation of early Christians, the sense that the end of the world was at hand and the Second Coming of Christ was expected at any time. In Syriac Christianity there is a strong sense of living like the angels. Recalling Matthew 22:30, they interpreted living like angels to mean living celibately, since Scripture said that in heaven we would neither give nor take in marriage but are like the angels. Celibacy prefigured immortality, when procreation would not be necessary since there would be death no more. There was a mind-set that if one could live now, in this present dispensation, as one would live then, one could hasten the coming of the new world.[48] Christ was the Heavenly Bridegroom to whom the believer was betrothed. The redeeming work of Christ, the Second Adam, brought salvation to humanity and the promise of a return to Paradise.[49]

Superimposing the Marys

The question of when the replacement of the Magdalene by the Virgin began to occur has not been fully answered as far as I know, though the replacement is explicit in Ephrem by the fourth century. Scholar Robert Murray has concluded that the Syriac tradition "deliberately and systematically 'superimposed' the Maries."[50] If Murray is correct in suggesting a superimposition, we have an interesting and subtle phenomenon. In a superimposition, two figures or images are brought together with one placed over the other. In the process a new image is created out of what were originally two separate images. We could say that in the process of superimposition, a new image is created for Mary the Mother as apostolic witness to the resurrection, though in this creation, the Magdalene is superseded and lost, no longer significant as a leadership model.

Re-ordering the Mother and the Magdalene

What forces were at work here I must leave to the historians of the Syriac tradition, but so it was that Mary Magdalene by the fourth century was replaced in her apostolic seeing by the Virgin Mary. According to Murray, there were two lines that emerged in early Syriac Christianity: one line replaced the Magdalene with the Virgin Mary, as in Ephrem, and the other retained both Mary Magdalene and Mary the Mother at the tomb. Within this second line an early third-century work entitled in Syriac "Catholic Teaching of the Twelve Apostles and Holy Disciples of our Savior" is an example. In this work on church order we find an inversion of the wording of Matthew 27:61: from "Mary Magdalene and the other Mary were there, sitting opposite the tomb" to "Mary and the other Mary, Magdalene." If we have lamps in our hand, we can easily see a re-ordering of the two Marys had taken place. We might say that the Magdalene has been literally "othered." This line of the Syriac tradition of the two Marys at the tomb and their re-ordering finds its classical expression in the fifth-century Rabbula Gospels, in which the Virgin is portrayed as first witness to the resurrection. In a miniature entitled "Crucifixion and Resurrection," we have a glimpse into the way these events—and those who witnessed them—were understood in this region from the fifth century onward.

Fifth-Century Rabbula Gospels

At the top of this picture, there's a sun and moon overlooking the dramatic scene: Christ, haloed, is wearing a long tunic of purple with vertical stripes of gold. Also pictured are two thieves and two soldiers—one holding a lance and the other a sponge. Mary the mother of Jesus is in a posture of grief, haloed and dressed in a purple cloak; beside her is John, without a halo. On the right are three women. Who are they? But is this the right question when we consider a symbolic and liturgical expression? Mary Magdalene may be the first one—she's dressed in a dark yellow cloak and light violet tunic, raising her arm in grief. The other women may be Mary of Clopas and Salome.

This fifth-century miniature is one of the earliest depictions of the crucifixion and certainly one of the most complex. Below the crucifixion scene is the resurrection: A small temple with a door with square panels and a roof depicts the tomb. An angel in white sits on a block of stone and turns to two female figures moving toward the tomb. We see Mary again, haloed, encountering the angel, and another woman who might be Mary Magdalene. This time the Virgin, in violet, holds in her left hand a container of fragrant ointment and with her right hand makes a gesture of speech toward the angel. She has been given the role of Mary Magdalene as apostolic witness to the resurrection. The other woman, possibly Mary Magdalene, holds a censer for burning incense, whose flame and shape are the same as the censer the priest Zacharias holds when he encounters an angel in another miniature in the Gospels. As one art historian has asked, what does it mean to find a woman here with the censer symbolizing the altar?[51]

On the right are Mary the mother of Jesus and another woman encountering Jesus. The haloed Mary is in the pose that will be used in Western iconography for the "Don't cling to me" posture with which Mary Magdalene has for centuries been associated.[52]

Crucifixion and resurrection from fifth-century Rabbula Gospels (Folio 13 a [233] Biblioteca Medicea-Laurenziana, Florence, Italy).

Virginity and Apostleship

There are threads in Ephrem of the Magdalene, though they are "under" his commentary. There's an empowering of a woman as an apostle and a witness to the resurrection. There's a detail of a woman being mystically transported into another realm in the garden encounter [53] and an acceptance of the visionary experience in a way we don't find in the West. And we find in this Syriac tradition a reverence for nature and the interconnectedness of all elements and reflections that make abundant use of feminine imagery. Possibly Ephrem's replacement of the Magdalene with the Virgin did not emerge from a disrespect for the feminine or a disregard for the sacredness of nature. More probably, it sprang from a tendency to look for a type together with a high regard for celibacy and virginity that had taken hold so early in Syriac Christianity. In the writings of Ephrem, virginity clearly goes together with witness and apostleship.

8

❀

Breaking Out of Old Stories

Sorting through Commentaries
and Legends in the West

HOWEVER ENLIGHTENING MY ADVENTURES in Syria had been, I still wanted to reach back into history and preserve individuality for each of the Marys. My desire to discover the historical Magdalene in her own right was becoming more pressing. With the Magdalene energies leading me on to recover lost history, I turned back to the West where the Virgin and the prostitute had become opposite poles.

The image of the hapless Psyche sitting on the dungeon floor, sorting the wheat, barley, beans, and lentils into their proper heaps, floated into my head—as though there were some connection. Psyche had been banished by the powers that be after her attempt to see. The consequences were severe. She had seen what she was not supposed to see. Her "fair dwelling place" has disappeared. Left to herself, she is unable to move into her own experience. She turns to Aphrodite, who agrees to help her if she can complete a seemingly impossible task of sorting—and finish it all by twilight. And

Psyche's troubles are far from over when she finishes tidying up the beans. Aphrodite gives three more jobs—going out into the sheep pastures and gathering an armload of their golden fleece, catching clear water in a bowl from the craggy mountain tops, and descending into the netherworld to bring back beauty in a jar. Calamity after calamity befalls Psyche in her process of discernment as she slowly and persistently goes more deeply into her own heart and finds resources she didn't know she possessed. In the struggle, she creates new possibilities. In the end she finds her own humanity and divinity.

The sorting task is fit for the human soul. It's a project to test the powers of reason and diligence. In Lewis's retold tale, there's no anguish to be seen on Psyche's beautiful brow—and no despair, for the ants are helping her sort on that cavern floor.[54] Sorting through the commentaries of Western church leaders would be as arduous a task, a putting together again what had been mislabeled and lost. But as Psyche's commitment to the task led her to new discoveries, perhaps the ancient writings would create new openings about the Magdalene and ourselves.

In a flash I imagined Aphrodite (Venus) flying in on her chariot commanding me to the sorting task. For the sake of the goddess of love, I laughed, I would continue to sort. After all, in the sorting process Psyche was breaking out of her own story as defined by her culture and religion. And something deeply transformational was going on for those of us in our community who were breaking out of the Magdalene's old story. It wasn't just about the Magdalene. It was about us. The first step of the breakout was realizing we had been "trapped in a script we didn't write," to use Carolyn Heilbrun's words.[55]

In Lewis, Psyche's sister finds herself in the same plight of sifting and sorting. Her labor takes place in her writing that overflows into her sleep. She explains it as "separating motive from motive and both from pretext."[56] This was good advice: the sorting brings motives to the foreground in this seemingly impossible task, separating out the real motives from the pretended ones. The sorting could move us out of ignorance into more love.

Luke's Sinner

The most crucial matter in reading the Western leaders is to differentiate Mary Magdalene from the woman in Luke's story "who was a sinner," generally understood to be a sexual sinner, or prostitute. Margaret Starbird has helped us get out from under the label of prostitute in the biblical story by attending carefully to the use of the word "sinner," which in Greek (*hamartalos*) is not synonymous with "prostitute" (*porni*) in the first place. Luke's word has a more general meaning of someone who has avoided an obligation or has been dishonest in a business transaction. But as Starbird rightly says, the notion of the prostitute caught on and sexual connotations flourished in history and art, and Mary Magdalene, who became fused with Luke's sinner, was depicted as sensual and ravishing, dressed in scarlet with flowing strawberry blonde hair.[57] The Magdalene, in this reincarnation, becomes the beautiful but sensual soul of Christianity, with all its woes, sitting on the cavernous floor, in the desert wilderness, repenting of sins.

As Luke tells the story, the sinful woman enters the house of the Pharisee with "an alabaster jar of ointment."

> She stood behind him [Jesus] at his feet, weeping, and began to bathe his feet with her tears and to dry them with her hair. Then she continued kissing his feet and anointing them with the ointment. Now when the Pharisee who had invited him saw it, he said to himself, "If this man were a prophet, he would have known who and what kind of woman this is who is touching him—that she is a sinner." (Luke 7:38–39)

Here in this last section of Luke 7 was a grain of wheat or a bean (found in two words "sinner" and "touch") that irresistibly leaped into what came next in Luke's story. In the beginning of what we now call chapter 8 is a description of the followers who had accompanied Jesus from Galilee. In this description Luke mentions what may have been three groups in his mind: the "twelve" and "some women" and "many others" as accompanying Jesus as he traveled, bringing the good news of the kingdom of God:

The twelve were with him, as well as some women who had been cured of evil spirits and infirmities: Mary, called Magdalene, from whom seven demons had gone out, and Joanna, the wife of Herod's steward Chuza, and Susana, and many others, who provided for them out of their resources. (Luke 8:1–3)

I knew this task of sorting was the precursor to all else. Between this last section in chapter 7 of Luke and the first section of chapter 8 that mentions Mary Magdalene was the interpretative move, linking what was taken as the sexual sins of one woman with the seven demons of another, putting them in one heap, and thus transforming Mary Magdalene into a sexual sinner from whom seven demons had gone out, where she resided in the hearts of men and women who called themselves followers of Jesus for at least 1,400 years. Beginning in the fourth century, the move had been made in some corners of the church, among the popular masses as well as by church leaders. In the sixth century the move was definitively set out by Pope Gregory I in a sermon in 591. Thus the mystery-laden Mary Magdalene, known for her patience and perseverance and loyalty to Jesus and for her visionary prophecy following her encounter with the risen Lord, was pushed into the darkness by her contrived sensational past. Her true light had almost gone out.

It's important to recall in this context the labels and disparaging remarks and insensitive words we use to describe people not belonging to "our group"—we falsely link undesirable character traits with "the other" groups. Getting out from under this kind of language abuse is a significant call in itself—if taken up, this call could lead to more reconciliation and a closer embrace among opposing peoples, nationalities, and creeds.

The Treasure of the Biblical Magdalene Story

There are only a few words attributed to Mary Magdalene in the Bible: her script can be found in the Gospel of John 20:1, 11–18. The treasure of her encounter with Jesus is found in verse 17, in which Jesus tells her that he is ascending and gives her a teaching to proclaim: "Do not hold on to me, because I have not yet ascended to the Father. But go to my brothers and say to them, 'I am ascending to my Father and your Father, to my God and your God.'" The verse retains vestiges of Mary Magdalene as a prophetic visionary whose experience is akin to Paul's experience on the road to Damascus.

Though interpretations of the passage vary, one Magdalene scholar, Esther de Boer, draws attention to the significance of the passage from within the context of the Gospel of John itself: the passage proclaims both the completion of Jesus' work and the culmination of the Gospel of John. For de Boer, the passage depicts a threshold moment between death and the implicit ascension. In the moment, Jesus gives Mary Magdalene a new revelation: she is the "sole witness of Jesus going upwards and the sole witness to his final revelation." In John's theology, the ascension of the Son of Man and the giving of the Spirit are intimately connected. These words announce the coming of the Holy Spirit that redefines discipleship. The disciples are no longer slaves to the master, but are brothers and sisters; my Father is your Father and my God your God.[58]

"Do Not Touch Me"

But in both commentaries and in art, by far the most remembered portion of this treasure are the words of Jesus "Don't hold onto me." Through the centuries, "Don't hold onto me"—originally *mi mou haptou* in Greek and rendered into Latin *noli me tangere*, has been translated as "do not touch me," or "do not cling to me," and variously interpreted. Even today, there's no consensus concerning the meaning of the phrase, and commentators continue to debate. In early church history it is the translation of the phrase as "do not touch me" that caused the most discussion about the Magdalene, especially when compared to the words of Jesus to Thomas, ten verses later: "Put your finger here and see my hands. Reach out your hand and put it in my side. Do not doubt but believe." Thomas answers Jesus, saying, "My Lord and my God!" and Jesus responds: "Have you believed because you have seen me? Blessed are those who have not seen and yet have come to believe" (John 20:27–29). Much of the discussion had concerned why Jesus tells Mary Magdalene *not* to touch and yet explicitly tells Thomas to touch. Here was another seed of a word beckoning for meaning.

Resurrection of the Body

The earliest Western fathers in the first few centuries showed some concern about the phrase "Don't touch [cling to] me," for its possible implication that Jesus' resurrection was not fully bodied. It was important as they presented Christianity to the Greco-Roman world of their day to verify that Jesus' resurrection was bodily. The sensory evidence supplied in the Thomas scene made that clear—Jesus asked Thomas to use his sight and his touch to verify his reality. The encounter with Mary Magdalene, on the other hand, seemed less useful as evidence of a bodily resurrection since Jesus asks her not to touch him.

These earliest fathers wanted to present the faith not as a mere subjective impression or an internal vision of resurrection. If the encounter with Mary Magdalene had been objective and real—if Jesus were standing before her in flesh and blood once again alive after the dying—why did Jesus ask her not to touch him? Making sense of this disparity was a conundrum and a concern, and while one church father found an unusual implication—that female and male ascetics should not live together—in general, the early fathers didn't criticize Mary Magdalene for Jesus' reticence to be touched.[59] That criticism was yet to come.

Fourth Century and Radical Change

By the fourth century the identity of Mary Magdalene in the West had moved into its radical change. It's significant that in the East Mary Magdalene was never understood as a penitent prostitute. Yet in the fourth century, in the writings of Ephrem, her role as witness to the resurrection had been given over to the Virgin Mary and the idea had been spread that the Magdalene was the woman whose demons had gone out.

In the West, Ambrose (339–97), the Bishop of Rome, beginning in 374 encouraged his listeners to "cling to Christ" in spite of Jesus' prohibition to Mary Magdalene not to do so. Citing Paul as his authority ("I permit no woman to teach or to have authority over a man; she is to keep silent" in 1 Timothy 2:12), Ambrose generalized the phrase from the Gospel of John with respect to women, interpreting "do not cling to me" as a prohibition against women teaching. Mary Magdalene had failed to recognize Jesus' heavenly state and didn't believe his divinity, Ambrose argued—it was a failure, he concluded, on her part. Augustine (354–430) agreed with Ambrose, though he couldn't resolve why Mary Magdalene wasn't allowed to touch Jesus while Thomas was.

Later fathers continued the notion that the phrase "Don't cling to me" indicated the Magdalene's inadequate understanding of the faith, and added that unlike Thomas, Mary was unworthy of touching Jesus. Her commission wasn't to proclaim the good news of resurrection, they concluded, but to go to the brothers so her weakness could be supplemented by their strength.

Twelfth-Century Interpretations

These interpretations continued into the twelfth century: Jesus' "do not" was taken a prohibition against women preaching and administering the sacraments. Women were not to take on important roles in the church, but to consult those who were more perfect. Even if the women in question were learned and holy, they were forbidden from handling sacred objects, vestments, and incense and to carry the consecrated host to the sick.

Pope Innocent III expressed similar views in a letter to two Spanish bishops on December 11, 1210:

> Recently certain news has been intimated to us, about which we marvel greatly, that abbesses . . . give blessings to their own nuns, and they also hear confessions of sins, and, reading the gospel, they presume to preach in public. This thing is inharmonious as well as absurd, and not to be tolerated by us. For that reason, by means of our discretion from apostolic writing, we order that it be

done no longer, and by apostolic authority to check it more firmly, for, although the Blessed Virgin Mary surpassed in dignity and in excellence all the Apostles, nevertheless, it was not to her but to them that the Lord entrusted the keys to the kingdom.

Twenty-four years later, Pope Gregory IX cited this letter in his *Decretals*, which had the force of law, and elsewhere he acted to prevent women from entering the sanctuary, serving at Mass, reading the gospel in public, acting as confessor, and preaching. At the same time, Thomas Aquinas, citing Paul and Ambrose as his authorities, argued against women's witness of the resurrection, since "it is preaching which makes this witness public and preaching is not a woman's function." The Roman legal tradition, which legislated against women giving public witness, informed his judgment as well.

This was when I began to see that the words of Jesus in the garden encounter with Mary Magdalene had gone around the bend and detoured into such an abyss that everyone seemed to have forgotten where they started. In the West, the church fathers seemed to have lost contact with the words they were misinterpreting. In their construction, the word "touch" was functioning in an extraordinary way, giving rise to absurd assumptions about what Jesus meant. Was there a problem with the very choice of the Greek word for "touch" or "cling," or the choice of its meaning? I began to think about this word and the context in which it arises and come to my own interpretation—as perhaps we all need to do. My interpretation leads back to the Aramaic, the original language of Jesus. Digging back to the original language helps to uncover in the word "cling" a fuller meaning.

Today we easily see the assumptions behind these prohibitions against women. They suppose a purity chain of being: God is perfect, and then follows man (men), then women, beasts, and so on down the ladder. Today, we choose to say no to these assumptions and all that falsely defines woman, and we choose to say no to the false assumptions about Mary Magdalene.

"Don't cling to me" has nothing to do with any imperfection, or sin, or demon within the Magdalene, nor any failure to grasp the resurrection faith. Quite the opposite: that the Magdalene envisions Jesus speaking in this way indicates the depth of her spiritual experience. Or as Ephrem said, when "Mary" recognized him, "she was transported in spirit to that other coming."

The words have nothing to do with her impurity or her female earthiness or any inappropriate embracing—she is not trying to hold Jesus back, as some commentators have intimated. Surely, the phrase about clinging has nothing to do with who is eligible to perform the sacraments, the preaching and teaching.

For me, the encounter between Jesus and the Magdalene is not all about Jesus, as we have often taken it to be. Jesus, her teacher, is thinking about *her* needs, not his own. Seeing her in the fullness of her humanity, made in the image of God, he calls her forth into the power of God that is within her, empowering her over a threshold that has been holding her back. He seems to be saying: *Go and tell the brothers of my ascent to my Father and your Father, to my God and your God. Don't cling to me in our earthly relationship, for I am ascending. Find your way of ascent. Find your path. Find yourself in God. You, too, may be united with the Glory.* It is a far different message than the one the Latin church fathers after the fourth century were proclaiming.

In truth, trying to keep a level head and be as charitable as possible to the Latin church fathers came to wrack and ruin for me at this point in my soul journey. So little value had been given to the Magdalene's spiritual experience and expression, and by twists and turns she had become a means of referring to evil and sinfulness in mind and body. My sorting was enough to let go of the tradition altogether—leave behind a tradition that changed the face of a revered apostle to an "untouchable" in a kind of caste system that was much more subtle than those caste systems that were declared openly within a culture. Yet, like Orual, Psyche's sister, I persevered in the sorting, separating motive from motive and both from pretext. I vowed to stay in the betwixt and between—as insider and outsider, a foot in both worlds and, I hoped, a bridge between the two.

The Legends

Then I turned to the legends that bring multiple problems to the sorting process. "No other biblical figure—including Judas and perhaps even Jesus himself—has had such a vivid and bizarre postbiblical life in the human imagination, in legend and in art," says noted Magdalene scholar Jane Schaberg.[60] We could say there is too little of her *and* too much of her in the Gospel narratives. Though she's an important figure at the resurrection, there's so little about her in the rest of the Gospels. This combination gives rise to the legendary.

The Gospels are utterly silent about Mary Magdalene's house and family—and the silence seems to have been an invitation for medieval preachers to simply invent a history for her. One preacher gave her an entirely fictitious lineage, asserting that Mary Magdalene's parents were named Eucharia and Theophilus, and that she came from the royal house of Israel; her father, in this scenario, was the governor of Syria and surrounding maritime territories.[61]

Besides inventing details about Mary Magdalene's life, storytellers also made a habit of borrowing details from the lives of characters actually mentioned in the Bible. Legends of the Magdalene regularly intertwined her story with that of Mary of Bethany, giving her two siblings: Martha and Lazarus, placing Lazarus and Martha in the house in Bethany and Mary in the *castellumn* of Magdala. Connotations about wealth in some instances accrued to her, perhaps taken from the general references to the women in three Gospels—though Luke is ambiguous about Mary's inclusion in this group—who "provided for [Jesus] when he was in Galilee" (Mark 15:41; Matthew 27:55; Luke 8:3)

Medieval preachers had their own moral commitments to various ideals of virtue. Whenever the Bible was silent on important points, they were not shy about filling in details in order to instruct their congregations. As a preacher, I understand the power of a good story for illustrating a point in the pulpit, and I know the temptation to stretch the truth as a means of making a point. But these "instructive" stories that medieval preachers used to give salt to their homilies further ensconced the Magdalene in her already solidified position in the Christian community as a prime example of female impropriety.

By the medieval period, Mary Magdalene's fusion with various women in the Bible—and her character as reformed prostitute—had crystallized into an unquestioned truth. The preachers as well as the people in the congregation, both women and men, assumed her devalued character. In some instances, they combined the fiction of her wealth with the fiction of her sexual sins. One preacher, for example, promoted the idea that it was her money that led to her downfall. Mary Magdalene, he preached, illustrated the consequences of the love of money, which led to "gluttony," "carnal concupiscence," and "carnal sin."[62]

Penitence and Preaching

The legends about Mary Magdalene that sprung up after she had been definitively declared a demon-filled prostitute by Pope Gregory in 591 usually include that assumed aspect of her character even when they simultaneously present her as an apostle, preaching and teaching in Gaul. Unlike James, whose character was not changed in the negative, or Mark, Mary Magdalene's "glory" had to do with her supposed conversion from the wayward and seamy side of life. Her glory had to do with her sexuality, which she was able to conquer through repentance and reformation. Once we become aware of this unconscionable alteration of her story, we have a lens through which we begin to see the church's attitude toward sex, and toward women, especially those with voice and a mission.

When I read about the Magdalene legends that developed in the medieval period in the West, I was struck how these weave together her preaching and her penitence, and I began to surmise that in those days the one was necessary for the other. Whether conscious or unconscious, the penitence undercut the preaching and the prophecy—nothing new in the history of religious traditions. As Schaberg has said, the story of the sinner negates the story of the prophetic voice and its authoritative message.[63] One of Mary Magdalene's legends recounts how, as a persecuted follower of Jesus, she escaped from Palestine in a rudderless boat. Drifting for some time, it washed ashore on the banks of southern France, where in Marseilles, she preached to the Gauls. Early on, this legend[64] was linked with another tale that relied on penitence for its fascination: how after converting many in Aix-en-Provence, Mary Magdalene took herself to a cave to live the life of a secluded penitent. There was something not quite right—and perhaps even pathological— about this legend of Mary as a hermit. It spoke of her remaining naked throughout her thirty years of contemplation with only her hair, which had grown down to her toes, for a covering. For me, this legend was the very last straw. When I read it, I gave up on legends altogether and threw away the book of her medieval images. I was out of the dark.

It was time again to reflect on old stories that weren't quite old enough and how they seem to us today. Some were filled with a moral agenda you might invent to teach a child. Some were transparently crazy-making. It was clear that teaching a lesson about sexual sinfulness was very important to medieval preachers. In these tales that protested far too much, the problem about the female body was always the Magdalene's problem. These so-called "old stories" were obviously not "old enough" to be historically true, but their effect on the spiritual lives of hundreds of generations staggers the imagination. In the East, apparent in the writings of Ephrem, it was virginity that melded itself together with the witness of "Mary." In the West it was repentant sensuality that emerged as the combination with the witness of the Magdalene. Both witnesses of the women were characterized by references to their sexual lives, which had enormous implications for Christian spirituality.

It was becoming clear to me that my tradition needed to tell another story about the body than the one the fictionalizations of Mary Magdalene told. Our attitudes about the sacredness of sexuality are changing, which may be one reason why *The Da Vinci Code* legend that Mary Magdalene and Jesus were married is so intriguing today.

The Re-emergence of Mary Magdalene Today

There has always been a mystique about Mary Magdalene, whether she was understood as an apostle of high moral character or as a reformed prostitute. There's always been a fascination with her relationship to Jesus, her preaching and teaching, and after the sixth century, her penitence. In the Middle Ages there was an outburst of mysterious attraction and veneration that in its intensity rivaled any saint. There seems to have been an insatiable desire to fill in the gaps and lost details of the life of the woman whose seven demons Jesus had cast out and who remained at the cross and went to the burial place and received first blessing from Jesus after his entombment.

Today, Mary Magdalene has surfaced again into public consciousness. This time, because of new discoveries and a developing scholarship, she's not a silent woman of the resurrection, with only a few lines of speech in the Bible. She's not a model of penitence constructed by church leaders nor the repentant preacher and contemplative of her many legends. This time we recognize her historical importance in the early communities; she comes to us in complexity, with vision and voice and mature spirit. Perhaps even more interestingly, this time we see her as ourselves and our potential for our imagining a new humanity.

In popular contemporary thought Mary Magdalene has been transformed from a repentant prostitute to the bride of Jesus and bearer of his child. She is the Holy Grail, the sacred feminine, the lost goddess, the womb and fertility. Most of the stir has been activated by Dan Brown's *The Da Vinci Code*. Its supposed quotes from Leonardo Da Vinci ("Blinding ignorance does mislead us. O Wretched mortals, open your eyes!") set us up to solve the mystery of the Grail—not where it is, but who it is. Two opposing characters—Sir Leigh Teabing and Robert Langdon—give Sophie, the young ingénue, some lessons in Christian history. And the lessons are not those we learned in Sunday School. They are lessons about how Genesis and the doctrine of original sin demonized the sacred feminine and began the subjugation of women, and about how the history of the Christian Church was an all too human political process. Jesus' supposed plan to leave the future of the church in the hands of Mary Magdalene was submerged and went underground. In the creativity of Dan Brown, fiction and history become so woven together that all we can say is that *The Da Vinci Code* makes a good action story. But whatever its historical merits—or lack thereof— the book brings Mary Magdalene into prominence as a symbol of womanhood and conjugal intimacy and piques our curiosity about new manuscript discoveries, including the Dead Sea Scrolls and the Coptic Scrolls discovered in 1945 at Nag Hammadi. Sophie, like most of us, has never heard of the Gospel of Mary, which was discovered in 1896 in a Cairo marketplace.[65]

Another popular author who assumes the marriage of Jesus and Mary Magdalene is Margaret Starbird. Her books *The Woman With the Alabaster Jar: Mary Magdalene and the Holy Grail* and *Mary Magdalene: Bride in Exile* are read by those particularly interested in the Lost Bride of Christianity.[66] For Starbird, the loss of the feminine has been disastrous for our culture, wounding both men and women. With the Magdalene in exile, we have been cut off from intuition and mysticism, from compassion and Eros in the Jungian sense of relatedness. And these are only some of the aspects of our humanity we have lost.[67] Another book, *Holy Blood, Holy Grail*, by Richard Leigh and Henry Lincoln, stands in the background of these books that tell us of a secret tradition that Mary Magdalene was Jesus' wife and carried his child.[68] And further evidence of our contemporary fascination with the Magdalene: a major publisher has recently released Lesa Bellevie's *The Complete Idiot's Guide to Mary Magdalene*.[69]

In our contemporary community we continually ask why the Magdalene has surfaced today. Is the energy swirling around these books and the recent movie of *The Da Vinci Code* just random entertainment—an action-filled script for an evening's pleasure? Or is there something more to be grasped by thinking about the Magdalene in a new way?

Imagining the Magdalene as Jesus' wife answers a need to find a biblical figure who can, finally, offer a model of sexuality and fertility and spirituality in healthy combination. This imaginative scenario, which tells us more about ourselves than it does about the historical Jesus and Mary Magdalene, stresses the humanity of Jesus as a married rabbi. It helps write a different story about the sacredness of the body in contrast to the story about the fear of the body that has abounded in received tradition. It encourages us to ponder how the fiction of *The Da Vinci Code*—and our response to it—connects to the more historical and biblical Mary Magdalene as present at the cross, the burial, and the resurrection as a visionary and apostle.

Many historians struggle with this popular view of a married Jesus and call it fictionalization. Yet the reality is that because of the popularity of this view, scholarship and popular imagination have come together. Mary Magdalene has become the subject of cover stories for news magazines and of special television programs, with scholars discussing *The Da Vinci Code*, the Gospel of Mary, and manuscripts from Nag Hammadi. A CNN one-hour special, "The Two Marys," presented insight from scholars and reviewed festivals in honor of both Mary the mother of Jesus and Mary Magdalene. Magdalene.org is a popular website with book suggestions, a gallery of images, articles by scholars Karen King and Margaret Starbird, and devotional materials from "conservative Christian" to "pagan magical." The public seems to have a limitless appetite for anything to do with Mary Magdalene, and it's changing their beliefs in subtle—and not-so-subtle—ways.

In the flurry of the thought that Jesus was married, subtle changes are taking place within us, especially about the humanness of Jesus and about the sacredness of sexuality and fertility. If the imaginative scenario is true, the Holy One of the Christian tradition is then married and no longer a model for the celibate life. While all this is felt to be a positive sign in some corners of the Christian imagination, there are many more corners that resist. All these corners are of interest to this book, but the one that holds special interest is the one representing the work of historians of early Christianity who say that as the wife of Jesus, Mary Magdalene is still not a figure in her own right.

9

Re-imagining Mary
Magdalene as Jewish
Visionary and Prophet

To re-imagine the historical and biblical Magdalene as a person in
her own right, let's begin at Magdala, where Mary Magdalene was
most probably born, working our way through her probable beginnings to her probable encounters with Jesus to her well-attested
loyalty at the cross, returning at last to the tomb, carefully distinguishing her portrait as we go according to how she is being viewed
and responded to by the four evangelists who tell her story.

That the historical and biblical Mary Magdalene was Jewish is
largely a consensus. One scholar argues for her Jewishness on the
basis that she was known as Mary of Magdala (the Jewish name of
her town) rather than Mary of Tarichea (the Greek name of the
same town).[70] Also, the Gospel of John, in an editorial note, says
that she speaks Hebrew—or Palestinian Aramaic—in the garden
encounter with Jesus.

Map of first-century Palestine. (Courtesy of Westminster John Knox Press.)

The reference to "Magdalene" is found in all four Gospels. Mark and Matthew introduce her into their stories as "Mary Magdalene" at the cross (Mark 15:40–41; Matthew 27:55–56). Luke introduces her earlier than Mark as "Mary, called Magdalene," adding to the account given by Mark that she was the one "from whom seven demons had gone out." Later at the tomb, Luke names her again as "Mary Magdalene," and we can infer she was one of the women at the cross (Luke 8:2–3; Luke 24:10–11). John invariably refers to her as "Mary Magdalene," standing "near the cross" rather than at some distance in the other three accounts, and at the tomb and at the garden alone (John 19:25; John 20:1, 18).

"Magdalene" is part of her name and historical identity, and acknowledgement of her as a person in her own right. It's generally understood that "Magdalene" refers to a particular place, presumably her birthplace, probably Magdala. Rabbinic literature mentions an ancient town Magdala under various names:[71] Magdal (meaning "citadel"), Migdal Sebayah (meaning "tower of dyers"), and Migdal Nunayah ("tower of fish")—located near Tiberias, near the Sea of Galilee, a town with cross-cultural currents. Scholars have reconstructed it as a place filled with oppression and injustice from 63 B.C.E., when the Roman empire incorporated the land of the Jews. In the early first century, when Mary Magdalene was born, it had become a place of relative stability and prosperity, trading its salted fish, fruits, and dyed fabrics with Syria, Judaea, and Egypt. Only twenty miles from Nazareth on the west bank of the Sea of Galilee, it wasn't far from Gennesaret, Capernaum, and Bethsaida-Julias, where Jesus walked.

A Name and a Birthplace

All we really know about the Magdalene's early life is her name and birthplace. We know from our own stories that birthplaces and cultural surroundings help to form character. We also know that going back to our birthplaces—our own, or those of our ancestors—can help us define our background and clarify the internal "sedimented layers" that formed us.[72]

The name Magdala is mentioned in some ancient Gospel texts and not others. It appears in some manuscripts, not in those we normally use as sources for our modern Bibles, as a place called "Dalmanutha," where it's said Jesus and the disciples went by boat after feeding the four thousand (Mark 8:10). Some texts substitute Magdala or Mageda for "Dalmanutha," and we find Magdala and Magdalan substituted in some texts of Matthew for the region modern Bibles called "Magadan," where Jesus and the disciples are said to have arrived by boat after feeding the four thousand (Matthew 15:39).[73]

The reasons for substitution are unknown, but they do open the possibility that Magdala, Mageda, or Magdalan refers to the ancient town of Magdala near the Sea of Galilee. From this conjecture, we can imagine that Jesus and Mary Magdalene met in his early ministry in Galilee, where, according to Matthew, Mark, and Luke, Jesus' ministry began. He calls Simon and his brother Andrew, James and John, the sons of Zebedee, as they are casting their nets into the Sea of Galilee. We are told that Jesus left Nazareth and moved to Capernaum, a place only six miles away from our projected Magdala. The Gospel tradition tells us that Jesus teaches in the synagogues in Galilee and heals the sick, and that his fame spread throughout the surrounding region of Galilee.

Did his fame spread to Dalmanutha (Magdala or Mageda?) or to Magadan (Magdala and Magdalan?), where Mary Magdalene may have heard about him or may have seen him preach, in the synagogue in Magdala or in Capernaum? We cannot know. Did she hear that he'd been rejected in his own hometown of Nazareth, twenty miles away, having tied his mission to the prophet Isaiah's—proclaiming release to the captives, recovery of sight to the blind, and freedom to the oppressed? Did she hear of his exorcisms and healings? We simply cannot know.

The Bible doesn't mention her house or her family in Magdala, as it mentions those of Mary, Martha, and Lazarus of Bethany. It doesn't indicate that Jesus entered her house, as he entered the house of Simon Peter in Capernaum. All is silence with respect to her early childhood history.

We have no conversations between Jesus and Mary Magdalene in her early life before their encounter in the garden. We know much more about the encounters of Jesus with Mary and Martha. We know much more about the marital relationships of the Samaritan woman and the way Jesus empowered her as an evangelist to the Samaritans. But there's no recorded early meeting of Jesus and Mary: the only information about her early life is the brief and tantalizing remark by Luke that he adds to the tradition set forth by Mark that Jesus cured her of seven demons.

We have no stories of her childhood, but based on the evidence of her visionary experience as recounted in the Bible and in her Gospel of Mary, as a child she may well have become aware of her spiritual gifts and originality. She would have understood her gifts within her own tradition, its morning and evening prayers, its synagogue worship, the story of Sinai and the wilderness, the stories of the ancient prophets, who struggled to convey the word of the Lord.

Naming

Though the biblical Magdalene has been known through the centuries as "Mary," the Latin rendering of her name, she would have been known as "Mariam" by her contemporaries. Early texts, in fact, use "Mariam," rather than "Mary," when Jesus calls her by name in the garden encounter in the Gospel of John. The name "Mariam" would have been associated among Jewish Christians with the ancient prophet Miriam, who'd begun a woman's tradition of song and dance. As the sister of Aaron and Moses, she also had characteristics of a priest. The two names are equivalent: the name "Mariam" in the Greco-Roman world and "Miriam" in the Hebrew world are the same.[74]

Her namesake in her Jewish tradition was Miriam, the ancient prophet of the Exodus story. It seems reasonable to assume that the song of Miriam would have been part of her first-century childhood experiences. It seems likely that she would have heard Miriam's song at Passover and would have chanted along with the others the Song of the Sea. She would have rehearsed over and over again the remembered stories of the Israelites and their experience as strangers in a foreign land, of the liberation, and the protection of God. She might well have thought of herself as a stranger in her own town of Magdala, which at the time of her birth was largely dominated by the Romans.

If we could slip back into the fourth century or earlier and read from a text actually used in early Christian communities, we'd hear the story about "Mariam," rather than "Mary Magdalene." There

Miriam the Prophet and Woman. "Then Miriam the prophetess, Aaron's sister, took a timbrel in her hand, and all the women went out after her in dance with timbrels. And Miriam chanted for them: Sing to the Lord, for He has triumphed gloriously" (Exodus 15:20–21). (Permission granted for use: London, British Library, ADD. mS. 27210. folio 15 r.a.)

would be resonances with "Miriam" for the Jews in the community. If we imagine ourselves in an early community reading from an ancient copy of the Gospel of John on the day of resurrection, her story would go as follows: "Early on the first day of the week, while it was still dark, Mariam came to the tomb and saw that the stone had been removed from the tomb." After hearing Simon Peter's story and that of the beloved disciple who raced to the tomb, our reader would take us more deeply into Mariam's story.

> [But] Mariam stood weeping outside the tomb. As she wept, she bent over to look into the tomb; and she saw two angels in white, sitting where the body of Jesus had been lying, one at the head and the other at the feet. They said to her, "Woman, why are you weeping?" She said to them, "They have taken away my Lord, and I do not know where they have laid him." When she had said this, she turned around and saw Jesus standing there, but she did not know that it was Jesus. Jesus said to her, "Woman, why are you weeping? Whom are you looking for?" Supposing him to be the gardener, she said to him, "Sir, if you have carried him away, tell me where you have laid him, and I will take him away." Jesus said to her, "Mariam!" She turned and said to him in Hebrew, "Rabbouni!" (which means Teacher). Jesus said to her, "Do not hold on to me, because I have not yet ascended to the Father. But go to my brothers and say to them, 'I am ascending to my Father and your Father, to my God and your God.'" Mary Magdalene went and announced to the disciples, "I have seen the Lord"; and she told them that he had said these things to her" (John 20: 11–18).[75]

Breaking Out of European Centricity

Changing the name from the Latinate/European Mary Magdalene by replacing "Mary" with "Mariam" is no trivial change. It places Mariam and Jesus more clearly within a historical context of first-century Judaism, breaking away from European centricity. For those of us in the Christian tradition who identify closely with Mariam, it connects our spirits more deeply to the Semitic tradition and gives a fresh start in re-reading received tradition. After all the anti-Semitic remarks in the Christian Scriptures and tradition that have worked their way into the hearts and minds of children growing up, after all the oppositional thinking between Christians and Jews paraded in getting the Christian message across, we begin anew. Sorting through all the information and gathering threads to find the Magdalene's Jewish roots is a place to start.

The more we study the Magdalene, the more we realize she's a bridge figure for today. As a Middle Eastern Jewish mystic mediating the Divine, she stands in the tensions between Judaism and Christianity. As a figure in both canonical and extracanonical Christian texts, she stands in the tensions between the Biblical tradition and its lost spiritualities. There is something interesting, yet devastating, about a figure that stands in the between, on the borders between separations. Yet Mary Magdalene stands there in an open space filled with potential for forming a new humanity. Her story can show us how we create separations in the first place.

We imaginatively sit in the Magdalene's place at the table with Jesus and the other disciples—the Jewish fishermen, tax collectors, and women from Galilee. We visualize knowing Jesus and thinking through Aramaic eyes. We feel for ourselves the power of the spirit in Jesus, and we feel being included. His eyes move as easily from those of Peter, James, and John, and Nathaniel and Philip, as they do to Levi's eyes, the despised tax collector, and to the eyes of the women. All of us, without exception, are included in this fellowship, on the road, and at the crossing of every path.

What turns, we wonder, would the conversation take? It's easy for us to hear Jesus saying that the kingdom of God is drawing near. The kingdom of God is as near as yourself, the divinity of God is within you. Look within, says the Gospel of Mary, to find God.

Can Rosamond receive the bread? If we think back to the Magdalene, she can. She is one of us at the table before rules and regulations came to be. There are no doctrines or dogmas in Rosamond's mind—she is a pristine follower of Jesus communing with the sacred she finds in him.

The historical separation of Judaism and Christianity was much more gradual than the canonical Gospels lead us to believe—it hadn't been accomplished in practice by the early part of the second century, even though early church writers like Ignatius of Antioch speak rashly and violently against Judaism. Some followers of Jesus continued to worship in the synagogues on the Sabbath while also attending resurrection day services in their new Jesus movement communities. Shared worship continued in some circles until the fourth century, when the definitive separation clouded over the original belonging and the legacy of two separate religions was cast in church documents and decisions. It was a period of diverse and deep reflection. When we think ourselves back to this time,[76] we free ourselves of the stereotyping and the prejudice and the condemnation of "the other" that have crept into the church over the millennia.

And consider this: Jesus didn't think of himself as founder of a new religion but as a Jew with a mission to the people of Israel. His activity in Palestine is better understood as part of Jewish history and his movement as one of several messianic and apocalyptic movements taking place at that time.

The Magdalene as a Reconciling Presence

In our contemporary Magdalene community, it's difficult to imagine, from her portrait in the Gospel of Mary, that the Magdalene opposed groups that diverged from her thinking. In her Gospel, she is a reconciling presence when conflict in the community arises. It's easier to believe she moved without confrontation among those with different ways of thinking. In our community, we see her standing in the breech between opposing forces. It seems likely that she never separated herself from her Jewish roots, but it's also clear from second- and third-century documents that her witness was welcomed outside Jerusalem among non-Jewish folk.

Magdalene scholar Jane Schaberg has re-imagined Mary Magdalene within prophetic Judaism. Based on the word "ascending" in the garden encounter, she traces the Magdalene to the prophet Elisha who received the mantle from Elijah. Her interpretation places Jesus within a tradition of Elijah Christology, and the Magdalene as his prophetic successor. Schaberg underlines that Magdala has associations with the prophet Ezekiel whose vision of God's throne as a chariot was formative to early Jewish mystical practices. Magdala is also the place where the charismatic and spirit-led daughters of Job were buried.[77]

Magdalene Christianity

Schaberg has forged a new question: What would an early community inspired by the prophetic ministry of Mary Magdalene have looked like? Schaberg, whose work has influenced the formation of our contemporary Magdalene community, has given the name "Magdalene christianity" to an early egalitarian form of christianity that *actually* existed and flowed through the first four centuries C.E. (She uses a lowercase "c" because it was lost and not integrated into what became Christianity.) Though Schaberg's "sketch" of Magdalene christianity is "speculative, tentative, explorative, searching, full of (untyped) question marks,"[78] she points to aspects by connecting the dots between the Gospel women, the women prophets in the early church, and Mary Magdalene in the Gospel of Mary.[79]

But what made Magdalene christianity remarkable?

Schaberg says it was the emphasis on the resurrection. The women who had experienced the violence and the injustice of the death of Jesus at the cross later, after the burial, went to the tomb to care for his body. And following the mystical events there, they expressed a resurrection faith that became central to their spirituality. The resurrection, they insisted, can be experienced in this life as much as in the life to come, and they built a lifestyle based on that claim. For these women, and those they inspired long after them, to live the resurrected life in the here-and-now was to live a life that moved "beyond the deaths of division, and beyond the fear of death." Resurrection for them stressed "connection, interconnectedness, lives challenging boundaries and barriers."[80]

In Magdalene christianity, baptism would have been understood as clothing oneself in perfect humanity and linked to a program of social justice. Perhaps the imagery of the baptism of fire as expressed by John the Baptist would have been central within the community whereby the initiate clothed himself or herself with the holy fire of true humanity, the legacy given over to the community by Jesus. The baptismal ritual may have included the words that pre-date the theology of the apostle Paul, from Galatians 3:27–28: "As many of you who were baptized into Christ have clothed yourselves with Christ. There is no longer Jew or Greek, there is no longer slave or free, there is no longer male and female; for all of you are one in Christ Jesus." The "oneness" in Christ was "a stand against dispari-ties, barriers, cleavages, false distinctions, hierarchies, and differences that divided slave and free, Jew from Greek, men from women."[81] Magdalene christianity would have rejected all structures of domi-nation, all social, cultural, religious, national, and biological gender divisions and status differences"[82] and resisted the split between Judaism and Christianity.

In Schaberg's sketch, those inspired by the Magdalene would have understood the message of Jesus in different ways from the way Peter and Paul had understood the message. The celebration of the Eucharist would have been an expression of solidarity and connection rather than a representation of the death of Jesus and sacrifice. They would have celebrated the Passover freedom and Easter liberation. Egalitarianism in the community would have been central, and solidarity with the poor and the mistreated a major commitment. The women in these communities would have spoken as boldly as the men, slaves as boldly as free persons, and with an authority they received from their experience of the Spirit.

A Lost Community

This form of egalitarian community, Schaberg says, was opposed at every stage that can be reconstructed historically. It was almost com-pletely lost. With its erasure from memory came the loss of prophecy and leadership of women and its concept of Jesus as the Human One. Gone also were the importance of the wisdom and mystical tradi-tions and the understanding of baptism as challenging social inequities and barriers, along with the heritage of Mary Magdalene and the experience that resurrection of the dead is in some way the resurrection of the living. The community disappeared because of even more ancient—and petty—reasons: the desire to protect status, fears, jealousies, misunderstanding, ignorance, and politics.[83]

10

Re-imagining Mary Magdalene as Apostle of Love and Mystical Experience

MY HUSBAND KEN AND I had a lively conversation on a road trip one Sunday afternoon. The news of violence across the globe that week had been particularly terrifying. We began to wonder if it were true, as some have begun to say, that we are indeed looking at the end of history, the last days of this planet. We broke through the gloom in our conversation when we laughingly suggested we might first consider getting rid of our own internal histories altogether and taking ourselves back to zero.[84]

Of course we cannot get rid of history and the streams of thought and feeling that we as a twenty-first century people have been born into. We cannot begin history anew. Yet we can come to see, as Elisabeth Schüssler Fiorenza has said about the Magdalene, where our tracks went wrong, and where the trouble began.[85] We can take our torches to blast our "sedimented layers"[86] that continue to add to the violence and abuse. We can practice the un-saying of the Magdalene in her penitent disguise.[87] We can break out of old stories and simply say it isn't so. We can sort through the layers of language in which the story of the Magdalene is cloaked.

The language of Jesus, the Aramaic, for instance, absorbed into the Greek in the New Testament, creates a space between what Jesus originally said in his own language and what the early church said (in Greek) that Jesus said. Standing in that open space filled with potential, we begin anew to develop a true humanity.

Aramaic Roots

Reaching back to the Aramaic from the Greek is important to understanding the relationship between Jesus and Mary Magdalene. For example, the word we have traditionally translated as "touch" in the famous encounter in the garden can be traced back to the Hebrew and Aramaic word meaning "cling." This is an important return to a word used in the actual language of Jesus. The word in Hebrew and Aramaic carries layers of physical and spiritual and mystical meaning involving relationships. It is the word in Hebrew and Aramaic used in the second creation story in Genesis where it is said that a man is to leave his parents and cleave to his wife. It is the same word that is used in mystical Judaism to describe an experience of inseparable attachment in prayer and meditation between the human and the divine. Reaching back to the Aramaic and Hebrew opens a space for a fresh and a multiple-layered interpretation of the dialogue between Jesus and Mariam.

Scholars are actively involved in this study of original language. Through language study they are beginning to sort out the priorities that belonged to Jesus' mission and those that began to take precedence in the decades of the evangelists. Scholars are beginning to understand the difference in the structures of the Greek language that makes sharp distinctions and the less antithetical structures of Aramaic.[88]

Aramaic *Dev* and Hebrew *Devekuth*

In 1925 the scholar B. Violet[89] pointed out that if we trace the word we have translated as "touch" back to its Aramaic root *dev* and the Hebrew word *devekuth*, we'll have a better explanation of this enigmatic passage, "Don't touch me." Violet proposes that we trans-late the phrase more in accordance with its Hebrew and Aramaic root as "do not join me," "don't attach yourself to me," "don't cleave [cling] to me," or "don't follow me." Violet continues that the translation of the negative phrase as "don't follow me" gives us a clear positive in the mission given to the Magdalene as in "go your own path."

It seems to me that we have extraordinary possibilities here if we focus on the possible translation of the root word as "don't cleave [cling] to me" or "don't attach (or glue) yourself to me." This trans-lation gives a positive mission to the Magdalene in keeping with the mystery to which the word *devekuth* refers, not only in early Jewish mysticism but in subsequent mystical thought. Gershom Scholem, who has written extensively on Jewish mysticism, says that for Jewish mystics, the term *devekuth* expressed at once the sense of distance and the closeness between God and humanity: the term means "adhesion" or "being joined" to God. It is the word used by Jewish mystics with a certain psychological disposition toward the visionary. *Devekuth* is regarded as "the ultimate goal of religious perfection" and it's also found in the thinking of Christian and Islamic mystics. One fourteenth-century Spanish Kabbalist said: "He who is vouchsafed the entry into the mystery of adhesion to God, *devekuth*, attains to the mystery of equanimity . . . and from there he comes to the holy Spirit and to prophecy." Similar ideas have been expressed in Hasidism and Sufism and by the Christian mystic Meister Eckhart.[90]

We find the same root for the word used in Genesis 2:24, when a man is said to leave his mother and father and cleave (with its mean-ings of cling, join, attach oneself as glue, and with loyalty) to his wife. There are mystical connotations to words rooted in *dev* as well. In Judaism, conjugal intimacy has often been thought of as an anal-ogy for the close intimacy of mystical experience (ascent to) of God.

Consider this: Mary Magdalene, who comes to the tomb, is seeking to care for the body of her beloved. Jesus comes to her in a vision that reconfirms the reality of his ascent and continuing life, declaring that their former relationship as husband and wife has drawn to a close. Don't cleave to me as in our earthly relationship but go your own path and tell the brothers that I am ascending to my God and to your God. The negative command not to cleave to Jesus seems to have a clear alternative—while their former relationship of cleaving to one another as husband and wife is over, Mary's own mystical relationship to the Father is now unfolding. Jesus seems to be implicitly saying: our earthly love relationship has prepared you for the mystical and contemplative relationship with God, a relationship that also looks to union for its consummation. You, too, may be united with the glory. With this interpretation, the words "don't cleave [cling] to me" suggest a former relationship of married life within Jewish tradition. Because the earthly relationship is no longer possible following the death of Jesus, the earthly relationship has become an analogy for the spiritual relationship between human beings and God. Embedded in this passage, interpreted from within a context of Aramiac and Hebrew roots, the language of loyalty and devotion taken on with the wedding vows is applied to the loyalty and devotion to God. Here we have the beginning of a mystical theology that draws upon the intimacy of the married state as an analogy for the intimacy of one's relationship to God. The Song of Songs stands in the background—an intuition that the church fathers drew upon in their discussion of Mary Magdalene.

For me, this is a fascinating possibility. Like Margaret Starbird,[91] I had no intention of suggesting that Jesus and Mary Magdalene were married, and I'm not making any such claim here—language analysis is beyond my expertise. But for me, this intimates— though it doesn't prove—that Jesus and Mary Magdalene had been joined together as man and wife and are speaking in the garden the language of early Jewish mysticism about ascent and union with the Glory.

The garden encounter—and the enigmatic command of Jesus—is an empowering event for the Magdalene that sets her free from her burden of grief. Jesus is thinking less about himself than about her, and us, and the words and the experience move her into prophetic voice. Perhaps the Magdalene hears Jesus saying that she and the other disciples may too enter into mystery of ascent and *devekuth*: Don't cleave to me but find your path of ascent and *devekuth*. My Father is your Father, my God is your God. Perhaps the community that authored the Gospel of Mary in the early part of the second century understood the passage as saying something like: Don't cleave to me, for the Son of Man now dwells in you. This is a divine force we share.

But what seems even more important than intimations in this passage that Jesus and Mary Magdalene may have been married is that the possible interpretation calls us to confront our own views about sexuality and its sacredness. If Jesus and Mary Magdalene were married, it certainly brings sexuality back to its sacredness that it has lost for thousands of years. As Leloup says, if Jesus were married, sexuality is then redeemed[92]—something sorely needed in our era.

Scholar Esther de Boer sees a kinship between Mary Magdalene and Jesus rather than a marriage. She finds in the Gospel of John a portrait of the Magdalene as belonging to a group of relatives to Jesus, and suggests that the Magdalene was either a sister-in-law or a niece of Jesus' mother. Mary Magdalene goes to the tomb to care for the body and receives comfort in close proximity as a relative. In the garden encounter he calls her by name and her response as Rabbouni suggests the intimacy of a kinship.[93] Another scholar, Marvin Meyer, says while a reasonable case can be made that Jesus and Mary Magdalene may have been married, their love expressed in the Gospel of John seems more platonic and spiritual than physical. Perhaps they were married, perhaps not. We do not know.

11

Seeing Is Believing

MY SISTER-IN-LAW ANNE called late one evening. I responded to the tremor in her voice by grasping more tightly the telephone receiver—something, I knew, was very wrong. Anne said she didn't know how to tell me this, but my brother George had died. His death had been sudden: a heart attack just as he and his daughter Marie returned from fitting the tuxedo he was to wear for her wedding. George was lovable and humorous—downright funny—but still formal and stately. At a commanding height of six-feet-seven, all eyes turned to him, and for those who knew him, their heart gravitated toward him when he came into the room. Now he was gone. That was it. I would attend the funeral two days later.

I fell into a grief with which I was well-acquainted, having lost my other family members before and having served as a pastor to many in the last stage of life. Equipped with pastoral training, I became both pastor and pastored, recalling the stages of grief—the shock, the anger, the hoped-for consolation.

I'd somehow known the moment my mother left this earth, though I was far from her bedside. But I hadn't had the same knowing with George, though he'd been dwelling in my thoughts for some months before. Could it be that our connections run so deep that sometimes we do know these things, not only about ourselves but about others?

George lived in Princeton, so it would take time for me to be with his family—Anne and the four children, Anne Elizabeth, John, Marie, and George. The unexpected tragedy would consume my feelings and thoughts as I made preparations to fly from Texas to New Jersey.

Sometime in the between I was gifted with an image—a representation of George that came to me in a flash of awareness. In an instant, his smiling face was before me, looking into my eyes, just as jovial as he was in this life. He was dressed formally in a red tuxedo and seemed to be saying he was happy. Though I heard no words, the encounter seemed like a conversation. Perhaps he called my name, but I couldn't say for sure. Then he was gone. But in the process I had changed with this hoped-for consolation. I had moved to another dimension not seen with ordinary eyes and into a greater sense of accepting my intuitions about living and dying. I've wondered since if this is what C. S. Lewis meant when he had Psyche call her sister Orual to cross over the threshold and into the steps of her soul-house that some call only a dream, but for Psyche was a reality. I would like to think I lived for a moment in an overlap between ordinary perception and another seeing. However you explain it, for me it was a seeing that was a believing.

After the vision, I began to think of my spiritual connections with the color red: the Pentecost tongues of fire and the liturgical color we use when we sing, "Come Holy Spirit." The red door to the chapel at St. John the Divine in Houston and the red needlepoint stole that my friend Margery gave me for my ordination. Mother had always told me that red was my best color. Now it was clear to me that it was everyone's best color. Red formal wear was not inappropriate, and the red tuxedo George wore in my vision made perfect sense: George had joined with the Glory at the wedding feast.

On another flight, I was reading the *The Gospel of Mary Magdalene* by Jean-Yves Leloup. In a foreword to the book, the philosopher Jacob Needleman says that the central teaching of the Gospel of Mary is to sensitize us to "a spiritual teaching that sounds a call from above that also calls to us from within ourselves. The immensity of Christianity takes its interior meaning as a sign of immensity within the self of every human being." Needleman elaborates on the notion of *nous*, or mind, that Jesus speaks of when Mary Magdalene in the Gospel of Mary asks about those events "when someone meets you in a moment of vision."

> We are speaking of an unknown part of ourselves, which is at the same time the essential part of ourselves: the Teacher within, our genuine identity. The *way*—and it is surely the way that is offered by all the spiritual traditions of the world—is the practice, and the community supporting the practice, that opens a relationship between our everyday sense of self and the Self, or Spirit.
>
> It is in this miraculous yet lawful mediating contact between the higher and the lower within ourselves that the deeper, intimate experience of conscious love is given—a conscious love for our starved and confused self that is at the same time love for our neighbor whose inner condition of metaphysical poverty is identical to our own . . . this is the love that is spoken of in the words of Jesus, "Thou shalt love thy neighbor as thyself." It is a love that cannot be commanded, but that we are obliged to recognize as the defining attribute of our essential Self.[94]

Not for one moment, during the experience or afterward, did I ever take the representation of George as embodied in the sense I take people living in the world. And not for one moment did I take this image as mere fantasy and pure imagination. I believe it resided in a realm that Leloup speaks of, following Henry Corbin: in the Imaginal Realm which is in the between, between the sensory

world and the spiritual. It is to this Imaginal Realm, and to the
active imagination, that Mary Magdalene awakens us. For Leloup, it
is in this intermediary Imaginal Realm that Mary Magdalene has her
meetings with the resurrected Christ. Her visions are manifestations
of both body and spirit. Here we have gone beyond any walls
between the subjective and objective and into a realm where subjective and objective meet in an image or representation. Here we are
in a place of openness—"a place of meeting, confrontation, and
merging of subject and object known in their interdependence.
Reality is neither objective nor subjective; it is an inclusive third
state where the two imaginally become one."[95]

12

—❀—

Gathering the Golden Fleece from Medieval Mystics

SORTING THOUGH THE COMMENTARIES and the history and saying it isn't so is part of the process of dealing with layers. In Lewis's tale, *Till We Have Faces*, of the rational soul taking hold of itself when it discovers its own darkness, the sorting task is a prelude to Psyche's seeing her own human and divine face.

In the old mythology, as part of a continuing process, Psyche is commanded by Aphrodite to gather the golden fleece. She is to gather some of the wool from the fierce sheep. In the tale as told by Lewis, we see Psyche walking slowly and carefully along the hedge that borders the grassland, "scanning it like a gleaner, picking something out of it." Then we see bright golden flecks. The sheep had left some of their golden wool on the bushes as they raced past. This she was gleaning, handful after handful, into a rich harvest.[96]

Gathering the golden threads left hanging within a tradition is another part of the process of breaking out of old stories. We found in the baptistry in Dura-Europos a thread for reweaving the Magdalene tapestry—a bright golden fleck of light for clothing ourselves for our rebirth into a new humanity. The light is within us, if we can only see it. We moved across boundaries into the Syriac tradition to break out of a strictly European view. We found in Ephrem, hanging under the tradition of Mary the Mother, an affirmation of the visionary and apostolic character of the garden experience. Tracing the Magdalene back to the Jewish prophetic tradition and to the original language of Aramaic and Hebrew, we began to develop a mystical understanding of our love for God.

Rediscovering the threads that cherished the Magdalene in the medieval mystics is another way of gathering the golden fleece. Consider Marguerite Porete, a member of an independent and controversial religious community known as the Beguines in the fourteenth century. And consider Theresa of Avila in the fifteenth century. Then switch to another hemisphere and consider another ancient ruin of a non-European character for its truth and beauty.

Marguerite Porete and *The Mirror of Simple Souls*

When a storyteller weaves a tale that's repeated many times, it takes on a life of its own. Nearly a thousand years after Pope Gregory proclaimed in 591 that Mary Magdalene was a reformed sinner, and after hosts of writers had confused the Magdalene with Mary of Bethany and the woman taken in adultery, Marguerite Porete, writing in fourteenth-century Belgium, naturally assumed those stories to be true. But in *The Mirror of Simple Souls*, Marguerite gives the Magdalene a positive spin. Her view is a golden thread.

Marguerite retains the medieval confusion that Mary of Bethany and Mary Magdalene are one and the same person. She repeats the tradition that in the Mary and Martha story, it is Mary Magdalene, standing in the place of Mary of Bethany, who "has chosen the better part," a contemplative rather than an active way of living.

Marguerite, drawing from Luke 8:2, shifts the language somewhat when she speaks, in our translation, of the seven demons as "seven enemies." She also associates the Magdalene with the woman taken in adultery and the woman who washed Jesus' feet with her tears and dried them with her hair. For Marguerite, Mary Magdalene exemplifies the "repentant sinner."

Yet Marguerite's take on the Magdalene differs from that of the preachers. To her, Mary Magdalene carries no shame about her sins and no dishonor for the fact that her sins were made known before all people. She may be dishonored by those who condemn her, but within she did not concern herself.

Marguerite compares the supposed dishonor of Peter, who denied Jesus three times, and the dishonor of John, who fled from the capture of Jesus (Mark 14:51–52), to the so-called dishonor of the Magdalene. Her conclusion: like Peter, who didn't carry dishonor because he received great honor when he was blessed by a vision of the risen Christ, so the Magdalene, through her vision of the risen Christ, implicitly carries no dishonor because she too received great honor.[97]

Equanimity

Though Marguerite's argument depends on the assumption, which we today deny, that Mary Magdalene was a repentant sinner, it's important to note that she places Mary Magdalene alongside Peter and John and asks her readers to think of all three of them as worthy. Neither the Magdalene nor Peter nor John, Marguerite insists, had honor or dishonor, nor the wish to hide or conceal themselves. It is "of no concern to them that God might accomplish something through them, and for their sake and for the people, since it would be a divine work." Marguerite seems to be saying that Peter, John, and Mary Magdalene had "equanimity." The word "equanimity" is derived from *acquus* (even) and *animus* (spirit). When one has equanimity, we find in them a fairness of judgment and impartiality. There's a stability, undisturbed by agitating emotions, and not concerned with either praise or insult from others. It is close to the calm and the peace that the Magdalene in the Gospel of Mary radiates. It is close to the calm and stately grace represented in the figures of the women at Dura. (Marguerite

Porete came to an unhappy end in 1310 in Paris at the Place de Greve, burned at the stake as a heretic—her book, it was said, was "filled with errors and heresies.")

Theresa of Avila and *The Interior Castle*

Making our way through the hedges and gathering golden fleece, we come to Theresa of Avila. Her *The Interior Castle*, written in fifteenth-century Spain, provides stunning glimpses into the way Theresa understood the Magdalene. Though Theresa cannot transcend her medieval perspective and compare her own spiritual experiences with the Magdalene, it's different for us: with lamps in hand, we can sort through these experiences and gather up this rich golden fleece. For our contemporary Magdalene community, the seven steps in Theresa's *The Interior Castle* illuminate the seven spiritual steps of the vision of the Magdalene in the Gospel of Mary and help us transcend, forever, the negative conflations. Reading Theresa can help us appreciate more fully Mary Magdalene as the apostle of love and mystical experience.

To Theresa, the Magdalene, fused with Mary of Bethany, is the penitent sinner to whom Jesus says, "Go in peace." Theresa, like Marguerite, pairs the Magdalene with the other apostles, with both Paul and Peter. Paul and the Magdalene share the blessing of visionary experiences, while Peter and the Magdalene both knew the pain of separating themselves from God. "Since their love for God had grown so deep," she writes, "and they had received so many favors and come to know the grandeur and majesty of God, the remembrance of their misery would have been difficult to suffer, and they would have suffered it with tender sentiments."[98]

In *The Interior Castle*, Theresa compares the soul to a diamond or crystal castle with many rooms, just as in heaven there are many dwelling places. The soul of the "just person" is nothing else but a paradise in which the Lord finds his delight—for Theresa, nothing compares to the "magnificent beauty of a soul and its marvelous capacity." Theresa's thoughts are embedded in a language of metaphor and symbol: for her, the soul is the crystal palace, the Pearl of the Orient, the tree of life planted in the living waters of life.

The purpose of Theresa's *The Interior Castle* is to move her readers to recognize the sublime dignity and beauty of the soul and journey into it, rather than staying out in the courtyard, where the guards stay, unaware of the sublime loveliness within. This is the purpose of my book as well.

Theresa speaks of God granting Mary Magdalene and Paul special favors. The example of these favors shows how God grants favors to us. God can reveal his grandeur, she says, to whomever he wants. Sometimes he does so merely to show forth his Glory. He doesn't grant these favors because of the sanctity of the recipients but so "His Glory may be known, as we see in Saint Paul and the Magdalene, and that we might praise Him for His work in creatures."

The next reference to Mary Magdalene is important for our understanding *The Da Vinci Code* energy. This is the passage in which Theresa speaks of "spiritual marriage," the seventh and last step into the most interior of the soul where peace resides, where the soul and God are one.

Spiritual Marriage

Christian mystics throughout history have tried to express the experience of oneness that comes to them in their spiritual journey, often speaking of this journey as an ascent. For Theresa, the soul moves inward, into the center, where the Sun shines brightest and the light of illumination sheds its rays. The perspective in Theresa's writing is very much like that of the Gospel of Mary, imagining closeness to God as a process of moving into the interior of the soul rather than ascending up to a God who is "out there."

Theresa, along with many other mystics, has spoken of the relationship of oneness with the divine as a spousal relationship, finding in the oneness an inseparable loyalty and attachment. The oneness is analogous to the oneness of marriage hinted in the words from Genesis about leaving parents and cleaving to a spouse. This is the term we have been translating as clinging or cleaving, expressed as *devekut* in Jewish mystical thought and in other esoteric mysticisms.

For Theresa it is an experience of being completely within the soul where the human is at one with the divine. Eastern orthodox spiritualities speak of the soul's process of divinization, not in the sense that the human becomes God but that the human being has found an inseparable connection. This is spiritual marriage.

For Theresa, the experience of spiritual marriage is a knowing and insight. The experience happened to Theresa in a vision one day after she received communion. She likens the experience to that of the apostles when the risen Lord appeared to them and said, "Peace be with you." In Theresa's moment, Jesus told her that it was time that she considered "as her own" what belonged to him and that he would take care of "what was hers."

Here is a strand of golden fleece. I like to compare these words from Theresa's vision to Jesus' words to the Magdalene in the garden. Don't cling to me but consider *as your own* what belongs to me. Go your own path. I will take *care of what is yours.* The event speaks of interdependency, not dependency, of love and mutual respect. It encourages us to take care of each other in the same way. Embedded in this phrase for me is the insight of the ages that has been lost not only in relationships between men and women but between humans and the divine.

13

—✦—

Machu Picchu

MY HUSBAND AND I TRAVELED TO PERU, where we spent our first night in Lima. Walking there was hazardous, with its constant onrush of automobiles and its pollution from the car fumes that hung in the damp atmosphere of this coastal city. But despite the conditions, I felt comfortable in Lima, as though I sensed my ancestry went back to the ancient Peruvians. I thought of my Spanish teacher at Berlitz: she'd laughingly said she thought I'd been Hispanic in a former life.

As Ken and I walked through the streets, I began to imagine a different life story, the course my life might have taken had I been born in Lima, most probably into a Spanish-speaking Catholic family whose ancestry melded the Incan and the European.

Then we flew to Cusco and took the train through the Andes to Machu Picchu. Though I suffered from altitude sickness at the start of the train trip, by the time we arrived at Machu Picchu, several thousand feet lower from the 11,000 feet elevation of Cusco, I was feeling better. We took a two-hour tour of the ruins in the afternoon, then settled comfortably into our Sanctuary Lodge nearby.

We awakened at six the next morning to see the sunrise over Machu Picchu: a tourist tradition. But when we opened the shades and shutters of our small room, we immediately understood that no such viewing would be possible on this day. There was only enough light in the sky to make out the mist and gray clouds hovering over the mountain peaks. The sun was hiding her face behind the mysterious clouds, though we knew she was there for she dashed those clouds with streaks of white light.

In spite of the mist and drizzle, Ken and I decided to venture from the lodge to climb the agricultural terraces to a top vantage point. With the hoods of our parkas pulled way down over our heads, we started the trek. Ken speeded ahead of me, while I was slower and more deliberate—something in me kept pulling back the reins so that as I climbed I could look out over the Andes, still mostly covered with gray clouds. The clouds extended themselves in what seemed to be a slow and deliberate energy that descended into the crevices formed by the slopes of the mountains, covering over an area and then unexpectedly opening out a space. They began to play hide and seek, and I admired their cleverness, hiding an entire area of the sacred city with their arms of mist, then suddenly revealing a section of it. A mystery hung over the morning. Few tourists were up as early as we were; few were present for this blessing in the light rain and mist; few could hear the river way down below.

With every step upward on the stone steps, with every tap of the stick that shared the burden of my weight as I pulled one leg up, then the other, my experience of Machu Picchu deepened. I began to realize as I looked out over the sacred dwelling place of the Incas that here in front of me was a religious vision. The Incas who lived in these houses of stone and open windows had a way of seeing that I wanted as my own. It was cosmic and connecting, like the chapel space in Dura and the vision in the Gospel of Mary.

The Incas had chosen a place for their sacred dwelling from which the sky and the mountains and the river could not be ignored or displaced. No one could, unless they were blind or deaf—and perhaps even then it would be doubtful—no one in this environ- ment could be unaware of nature, its massive character, its awesome beauty and wonder.

One group of houses had been built so that the windows opened out to the place of the sun during the winter equinox, and another group of houses, the Temple of the Sun and the House of the Princes, opened out to the sun at the summer equinox. The build- ings had been deliberately accommodated to the environment with the movement of the sun and stars in mind. I wondered about the Moon and what it might have meant to them. The building came for protection, yes, from the harsh elements, and yet the building marked the spots in the environment that needed to be observed and examined and celebrated. Here, these people of the fifteenth century had built their lives around the activities of the Sun and Moon and rain and clouds and water. Here, in Machu Picchu was a strand of golden fleece. I wanted to take home to my own dwelling place and garden in Houston their vision, to open out more fully the draperies that covered the French doors to our garden.

Certainly the violence of the Incas had to be abandoned—the human sacrifice and the animal sacrifice. Catholic Spain repudiated the violence, but also it had dismissed the worship of the Sun, the vision of these people, who were as strange and different as Mary Magdalene had been. The Bishop of Cusco, and also of Lima, had intentionally placed the choir stalls in the *rear* of the newly built churches, rather than in their traditional place in the front, so that the Indian people could not look back at the Sun to worship during the Mass. The Franciscans and Dominicans had built churches on the foundation of Inca temples with all the certainty of a religious conviction that they knew what was right: "the other" was wrong. The Inca way of seeing had been rejected—their vision of human- ity's deep connection to the mountains and the clouds and the mist, their way of worshipping the Sun and the Moon and the stars the European priests thought had been misplaced.

The symbolic gesture of separating these people from the wor- ship of the Sun was today for me, at the top of our vantage point, a great pity that itself needed an un-saying. That Catholicism or any "ism" formed within Christianity needed to reclaim the cosmic vision of the Indian people was no longer a question, but rather one answer to a religion that wondered why it was no longer alive for so many. The agricultural and cosmic vision as part of the mystery of the universe needed to be reclaimed by Christians today.

In our travels, holy cities and temples had held a potential for spiritual experience for me—there was no question about that. There had been Borobudur in Java and hearing a Muslim crier calling to prayers those not going to the Buddhist temple as we were, and the story of the Buddha's vision recorded in the carving on both sides of the winding walkway that encircled Borobudur.

Yet Machu Picchu unexpectedly held for me the deepest synthesis in my developing Magdalene spirituality. Perhaps it was that we had more time here than in the other visits to temples and holy shrines, more time to absorb the experience. Perhaps it was so complete as a city, yet small enough for me to grasp its components as a whole. Or perhaps I'd reached a place in my own religious vision of thinking and imagining that God *is* the created universe and the mysterious More, and that I am *in* that universe and that God is in me. Whatever the reasons, I wanted to reclaim the cosmic vision of the Incas that was sorely missing in my religious tradition. I could look for those aspects in the Anglican prayer book that were often hidden from view. Retrieve those kernels for a rewriting of liturgy.

Why couldn't Christians reconnect themselves with the sacredness of all creation and experience themselves as a sacred part of that creation? To think that the human species had been separated from other species from which we derived I now saw as an old creation story that wasn't old enough. There would be no placement in my mind of choir stalls between my eyes at Mass and the Sun, the stars, the Moon, and the Earth. I was living matter as were the stars and the Sun. I was fiery material, as Hildegard had claimed in the twelfth century in Bingen. The whole creation had declared its divine energy to me and I could see my face.

14

Other Old Stories

THE BEGINNING STORY OF ROSAMOND remains unresolved. I've been thinking about it ever since, especially when Bill, a member of our community, remarked after a festival that celebrated Mary Magdalene, "There's a new paradigm of thinking going on here." I think his words are true, especially in the way we've begun to understand the relationship between the old stories of the Magdalene, our faith, and Jewish tradition.

Daniel Boyarin, a rabbi working in early history of rabbinic Judaism and emerging Christianity, and Karen King, who concentrates on the relationship between gnosticism and orthodox Christianity, have influenced my thinking about old stories. Understanding the Magdalene community as a connective community seeking conversation with other spiritualities and religious traditions grows from this way of thinking.

Conversations between Judaism and Christianity

First, let's take the old story of Christianity and Judaism as Daniel Boyarin has configured it.[99] One version of the old story is that Christianity developed out of orthodox rabbinic Judaism of the first century. There was a myth that went along with it: Judaism was the "mother" and Christianity the "daughter." From the viewpoint of Christianity, the daughter superseded the mother. From the side of Judaism, the daughter went astray.

Another configuration of the old story is that out of first-century Judaism and the destruction of the temple by the Romans in 70 C.E., two "daughter" religions were crystallized in the same era within the same background of enslavement and destruction. The two religions are now thought of as two sibling religions and are thus symbolized as the two sons of Rebecca, Jacob and Esau. But that raises another problem: which of the two will be identified with Judaism and which with Christianity? That depends, of course, on your point of view. Jews would contend that in the mythic metaphor, Jacob is Judaism and Esau is Rome; after 312 when Christianity was legalized by Constantine, the Christian Church, and Christians would contend the opposite, taking Jacob as Christianity and the elder son Esau as Judaism. Never mind how they get there.

But recent scholars have realized that these old stories and myths aren't old enough to be historically true. In the first place, there wasn't a first-century Judaism. Rather, there were many different Judaisms, with some twenty-four sects competing for the title of Judaism and the true interpretation of Torah. But Boyarin says only one sect was the seed for what became Christianity.

Likewise, there wasn't a single first-century Christianity, but many groups understanding the mission and ministry of Jesus in different ways. In the new paradigm and story the history of the first four centuries of early Christianity and Judaism are configured differently: Christianities were not separate and isolated from each other or from the diverse Judaisms, but were in struggle, in conversation, and in dialogue.

One scholar has given us this image to consider: today most of us consider Judaism and Christianity as two circles standing side by side, essentially self-contained religions. If we move back to the fourth century from today we see these two circles as separated from one another. But when we push further back into history, we see the circles begin to overlap. Going back from the fourth century to the first, we find an in-between space where meaning was shaped in the crisscrossing and in the conversation and in the struggle.[100]

If we think of the various meaning-giving groups as on a continuum, rather than as polar opposites, which they became when their separateness was articulated in the fourth century, we have a more realistic view of what the first four centuries of religious history in the Middle East and Europe must have been like.

Susanna Elm has cited a text from the *Historia Lausiaca* that describes a fourth-century Egyptian female ascetic who abstains and fasts to devote herself to prayer—except on Saturday and Sunday. That's because she observed both days as Holy Days, both the Sabbath and the Lord's day of resurrection.[101]

In those early days, one didn't necessarily define one's religious faith by negating another. Imagine, instead, people standing side by side, perhaps in the synagogue, or moving from one day of worship to the other, interacting with one another, and conversing with one another, disagreeing, listening, reflecting, and praying about what they heard. There would have been fuzziness about borders and distinctions in the popular imagination even though in certain arenas and in texts the differences might be pronounced and articulated. While there were surely differences among the groups, there would have been open conversations about them.

For us today, it may be helpful, as Boyarin suggests, to think of Judaism and Christianity as conversations rather than as completely separate religions. It may also be helpful to think of Islam and Christianity in the same way: as conversations about our true humanness and divine light rather than as completely separate religions.

Conversations between Christianities and Lost Communities

Another old story, according to Karen King, is that certain groups, after several decades of evangelistic and missionary preaching in the Christian community, began to deviate from the true teachings.[102] It was the old story of going astray. These groups, according to the old story, developed what came to be described as hidden and esoteric interpretations of the good news. They denigrated this world and were written for an elite group. A time came in church leadership when these interpretations were declared false and in need of a label that would reject them. These interpretations were named heretical and their teaching, heresy. To be a Christian was *not* to be a heretic but a believer in the orthodox teachings. In the old story, heterodox thinking became the enemy or "the other" against which "true" Christians defended themselves.

Church leaders, as Ignatius in Antioch, had taken the position that Christians were not to associate themselves with Jews. That to be a Christian was *not* to adhere to Judaism. The revelations of Christianity had surpassed those of Judaism. Christianity was now the true path. The same old story began anew within Christianity itself: church leaders took the position that Christians were not to associate themselves with those groups outside orthodoxy. In this version of the story, the outsiders had gone astray. Orthodox Christianity was the true path.

King and other scholars agree that this old story within Christianity is simply not old enough. It is far too simple, a story positing opposites and divisions and deviations. In the early years the labels were introduced by church fathers in forming what it meant to be Christian. These leaders formed what it meant by saying what it was *not*.

Historically it is more accurate to say there was a diversity of Christianities in the early complex process of Christian development. Various groups in the first and second centuries differed in thought forms and in ethnicities and localities. These various communities were interpreting the teachings of Jesus. To say one group was correct while the others were not, that one was true while the others were not, is far too simplistic and distorts true history. A far better picture of the first three hundred years of Christian history is that the different groups were in conversation with one another and were interacting with one another and that in that interaction meaning emerged. The community that authored the Gospel of Mary was one of those groups.

15

—❁—

Traces of a Lost Christianity in the Gospel of Mary

IT WAS TIME TO BUILD A COMMUNITY around the figure of Mary Magdalene. The words "A Community of Mary Magdalene the Apostle" kept ringing in my ears. We had been celebrating her festivals on an annual basis at the cathedral for eight years. We'd developed liturgies out of our own spirits rather than relying on traditional liturgies. We simply allowed our creativity to take over and express itself. It was the Magdalene attraction calling us forth. It was the Magdalene mystique. Now it was time to dig more deeply into ourselves and our lost memories and envision what a contemporary Magdalene community might look like.

Bridgitt, a member of our community, and I began to imagine our community meeting in a natural setting, among plants and trees, with only a minimal number of constructed objects to adorn the space: perhaps a bowl containing clear water or a candle or lamp that could be carried into the space, perhaps an unguent jar as a sign of the anointing of the Spirit. We would be looking for symbols of the water of life and the holy fire of true humanity—but all this was in process. Pam in our community was drawn to the quietness of Magdalene spirituality and imagined our practicing silence in our gatherings. We began to relate deeply to the passages from the Gospel of Mary when the descending and ascending soul of Mary ends her spiritual struggles in rest and says "I go now into Silence" and the gospeler adds, "Mary became silent, for it was in the silence that the Teacher spoke to her" (translation from Leloup). There was much we didn't know yet, as I suppose happens when one is creating something new, and in this case, something very old as well.

A group of us began to meet at the cathedral to envision a contemporary Magdalene community based on the work of Jane Schaberg and Magdalene christianity.[103] We intuitively grasped that our first step was to study the Magdalene's Gospel, mining it for what it could tell us about the teachings of Jesus and about the Magdalene, and about ourselves. These were the first days of our feeling the shared peace within. We were somehow being transformed into a community that understood what Jesus meant when he said, "Acquire my peace within yourselves." His teachings in Mary's Gospel were ancient though long forgotten—having been lost for 1,500 years—but they were fresh to our ears. For us, the study of the Gospel of Mary was life-changing. We had found a bright golden fleece.

We know that Mary Magdalene did not write the Gospel of Mary. We have nothing from her hand, as we do from Paul, for example. It would be from seventy to a hundred or more years after the death of Jesus that the authoring community of the Gospel of Mary gathered together. We can only assume that they gathered long after the Magdalene's death. We don't know what happened to the historical Magdalene after the death of Jesus and her visionary experiences of him—she is lost to us—though comments in church writings and legendary accounts give a range of possibilities to think about. Some say she remained in Jerusalem after the death and ascension of Jesus; others that she returned to her home in Magdala in Galilee or went to Ephesus with John and Mary the Mother. Still others believe that she was set adrift in a rudderless boat and landed in the south of France, and from there went to Egypt, or to Ethiopia. We do not know.

What we do know about the time of the writing of her Gospel is that Christianity had not yet emerged into orthodoxy. There is little in the Gospel we might call doctrine or dogma. Jesus is named the Savior and the Blessed One who teaches us to look within to find the shared peace. It was a time when the issue of woman's leadership in the church was being discussed. Leadership in some communities during this time rested on the inspiration of the Spirit rather than one's belonging to a particular gender, race, or class. In this Gospel the issue of woman's leadership is confronted openly and an answer is offered by Levi affirming the mystical and visionary leadership of the Magdalene who speaks boldly in the Spirit. And the second century was a time when the concept of the Human One was alive and the phrase "the kingdom of the Human One" was being used.

The Kingdom of the Human One

The community of the Gospel of Mary preached the message of the Human One that can be found within. We know this because in the Gospel, after the Savior has departed, the disciples ask the question in their distress, "How shall we go to the nations and preach the gospel of the kingdom of the Human One?" Or in another translation: "How shall we go to the nations and preach the gospel of the kingdom of the Son of Man?"[104] Or, as in another translation, "How are we going to go out to the rest of the world to announce the good news about the Realm of the child of true Humanity?" (King). The phrase "Son of Man" is translated by King as "child of true Humanity," not so much to modernize the translation as to be faithful to the inclusive use of the word *anthropos* that is used in the Greek. The kingdom of the Human One is for everyone, male or female, slave or free, Semitic or European, not for an elite. As Patty and Bill in our community say, for "absolutely everyone, without exception."

The women and men of the community of the Gospel of Mary must have felt gifted by the one they call the "Savior" and the "Blessed One." Also, they were inspired by the memory and spiritual maturity of the Magdalene. In the text, after the disciples ask the question about how they are to go out, it is Mary who stands up, embraces the disciples, and says to her brothers: "Do not weep and do not grieve and do not make two hearts, for his grace will be with you all and protect you. Rather let us praise his greatness, because he has prepared us. He has made us Human Being" (de Boer). Or in another translation: "He is calling upon us to become fully human [*Anthropos*." (Leloup). Or as in King's translation of the Greek fragment: "he has united us and made us true Human beings." De Boer's translation of "do not make two hearts" speaks to the sense of an internal conflict within that disturbs the potential for our living as true human beings.

At the close of the Gospel, in what sounds like baptismal words, Levi says, "Let us put on the perfect Human Being. Let us bring him forth to us, as he commanded us. Let us preach the Gospel, without laying down any other rule or law than the one the Savior said" (de Boer). Or "Let us become fully human [*Anthropos*], so that the Teacher can take root in us" (Leloup). Or "We should clothe ourselves with the perfect Human, acquire it for ourselves as he commanded us, and announce the good news, not laying down any other rule or law that differs from what the Savior said" (King).

The Gospel of Mary proclaims as a revelation from Jesus that the Human One resides within us. This is a divine force that is connecting rather than dividing. This gift of grace brings our divided selves back into wholeness and raises us to a love that is connecting, not rejecting. Love spreads, as light spreads. Love seeks others to love, takes people where they are, is not led by labels or stereotypes, doesn't assume the other has gone astray. From the perspective of the Gospel of Mary, the good news is that the Good (the Son of Man or the child of true Humanity) has come into the world and united us all as Human Beings. It is this divine force within that brings harmony within ourselves and in our relationships with others. We can find this true humanity if we seek it and if we look within. It is in a path inward into our humanness and divinity that we find the good news of the Gospel of Mary.

Resonances with Dura-Europas

Earlier we ventured into the discoveries at Dura-Euopas and looked closely at the painting of the women at the tomb. Those frescos that we think of as representing an early Christianity (232) were painted approximately a hundred years *after* the Gospel of Mary had been written down. So the Gospel of Mary records an even earlier understanding of the message of Jesus and the role of Mary Magdalene and her spiritual maturity.

I find resonances with the way the Magdalene is portrayed in her Gospel and the way she and the women are envisioned in the baptistry at Dura. The Dura-Europos women are calm, heroic, and holy. They have experienced the violence and injustice of the death of Jesus and have come to care for the body with their unguent jars. They venture in the second action into the subterranean darkness where the tomb is. They have come to *see*. They represent a new humanity being born into the water of life sanctified by the Good Shepherd. Their iconic presence recalls their transfiguring experience to the initiates who anticipate a similar experience in their clothing themselves with the Perfect Human.

The Magdalene in the Gospel of Mary seems to function in much the same way. She is a woman of vision with a compassionate and questioning, quick-minded spirit, not only one who experiences visions but one who asks the Blessed One about the nature of vision and the visionary experience. She has seen the Lord and has responded unwaveringly to the transfiguring experience that brings her to peace. In the Gospel she is the visionary of visionaries. Just as the central figure in the painting of the women gives focus to the space, it is Mary Magdalene that gives focus to her Gospel. After Jesus' departure she stands up to speak in his place, comforting and consoling the grieving disciples and calling them into the life of the Human One. She has moved beyond the fear of death and the departure of Jesus. She has understood the teaching that the shared peace is found within, if we seek it. She is able to move beyond differences and divisions and becomes a reconciling presence in the midst of a dispute that opens up in the community later in the Gospel.

We saw that in one interpretation, the space of the baptistry at Dura was a space of epiphany offering cosmic light and enlightenment to the initiates. In this understanding of the chapel space, light represents the nature of Christ. The Gospel of Mary begins with a message from Jesus about the interconnectedness of all elements in the cosmos and the goodness of nature. Later in the Gospel, when Mary's private revelation is revealed, we find Jesus teaching the soul how it might overcome the powers that dominate it. The first power in the revelation is darkness. The implication of the Gospel, though the pages of the text on this power are missing, is that if we recognize our true light within, we can overcome our own darkness.

The Gospel of Mary carries both a Greco-Roman and a Semitic character, as does the city of Dura-Europos. The Dura paintings in the synagogue and temples bring together without apology images from Rome and Persia. And the paintings in the Christian building are close, and yet unlike what we have in the Roman West. So it is with the Gospel of Mary, what we have is close, yet unlike what we find in the theology of the Roman West. Close, but unlike Paul—just enough to make a difference to us today. In the Gospel of Mary, clothing oneself in the Human One, as in a baptismal rite, is elevating and affirming. It speaks of our true humanity and divinity within. It is close but unlike the baptismal rite as it has come down to us from Paul, as a washing away of our sins and as a dying with Christ. In the Gospel of Mary we have crossed over a boundary into a legacy we see more clearly in the east.

For me the Gospel of Mary says in words what the paintings at Dura say in paint. Both extol the mystical and visionary experience as a path to connect to the sacred. Both connect to us as participants in the "seeing" in order to tell us something about ourselves. The Gospel, we could say, takes up the moment for which the women at Dura-Europos await. The disciples in the Gospel of Mary are actually experiencing the resurrected presence and revelation of Jesus. From the very beginning of the text that we have left to us, the disciples are in conversation and dialogue with the Savior and the Blessed One.

The Re-discovery of the Gospel of Mary

The story of the re-discovery of the Gospel of Mary is not as dramatic as Dura-Europos. And we know less about place and community than we know at Dura. We don't have solid ground to excavate to fill in the background, with temples and synagogues surrounding the site. We must rely upon the two Greek copies we have from the third century and the one Coptic copy from the fifth for nuances and meaning.[105] The fragment written in Coptic was discovered in 1896 in a Cairo marketplace by a German scholar named C. Rein-hardt. Coptic is a later development of ancient Egyptian hiero-glyphic script. As a living language it began to flourish in the second century C.E., but the copy we have discovered dates from the fifth century.

Two third-century fragments in Greek have been discovered. In 1938 another scholar, C.H. Roberts, discovered a small fragment of the Gospel of Mary within a collection of fragments that had been found in Oxyrhynchus, a city in Middle Egypt. In 1985 another Greek copy came to light, again in Oxyrhynchus. Interestingly, both Greek versions were found together with other sacred writings, some of which later became part of the Bible and others that were later excluded.[106] The second century was a time of conversation between a variety of views, with much interaction and discussion.

Though we can say from its use of Coptic that the Gospel of Mary was circulated and read in Egypt, this would not mean that it originated there. Karen King suggests that the Gospel was written in the early part of the second century in either Egypt or Syria. Another scholar favors Syria, since Levi plays a central role in Syrian writ-ings.[107] De Boer favors Asia Minor, perhaps Ephesus, not only because of the similar imagery she finds in the Gospel of Mary and in Paul's letters and the Gospel of John, but because Mary Magdalene is said to have been preaching the gospel there, where she later suffered

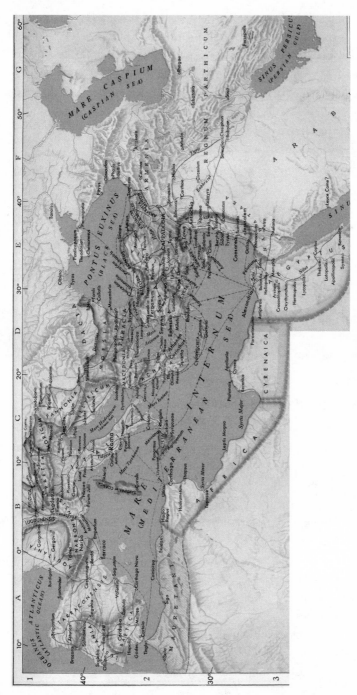

The Roman world at the birth of Jesus. (Courtesy of Westminster John Knox Press.)

martyrdom.[108] More generally, de Boer thinks that the Gospel could have been authored wherever Roman Stoicism flourished. De Boer has demonstrated that a Stoic perspective stands behind the Gospel of Mary. This view gives a positive view of the material world and the body. The Stoic perspective of the interconnectedness of all things in the cosmos is brought together with a Christian understanding of Jesus as the Human One that now dwells within the disciples. From this perspective, the Gospel is a Christianized Stoicism.

If the community authoring the Gospel lived in Egypt, Syria, or Asia Minor, it would have been a time in the early second century under the domination of Imperial Rome. These Christians would have gathered together to follow the teachings of Jesus. There may have been Jews in the community who read the Hebrew Scriptures in Greek. There may have been slaves and free, women and men, Greeks and barbarians, native Egyptians feeling the domination of both Greeks and Romans. It would have been a time when Roman Stoicism had filtered into the popular mind, for its teachings were for everyone, across the board, from the marginal to the mainstream Roman.

Resonances with Roman Stoicism

Roman Stoicism had been built on the more ancient teachings of Zeno. Some say Zeno wrote an alternative to Plato's *Republic* in which he envisioned a worldwide state whose citizens were not from Athens or any other particular place but from the universe. The state was patterned not after local traditions but after universal nature. There were no privileged persons in Zeno's thought, unlike Plato's *Republic* where there were philosopher kings and social and political elite. Zeno insisted that all were born free and equal. Furthermore, slavery was simply contrary to nature. "Women and slaves may become philosophers" said church father Lactantius in quoting from the Stoics.[109]

Zeno's utopian state had no laws (because there was no crime), no class system, and no hatred. Love was the master of this state. The wise human being, who was at once virtuous and possessed of spiritual well-being, was not a leader in our usual sense of the term but an ordinary citizen. Zeno's vision was to make the world a *cosmopolis* of wise and equal human beings living in harmony with one another and in tranquility within themselves. The moral life and the development of virtue was the responsibility and goal of human living. It was in the path inward, into self-knowledge, that virtue was attainable. Zeno loved poetry as well as logic, feeling and thinking, and had a deep reverence for the cosmos.

The Stoics taught a message about inner liberation, and they addressed themselves to all human beings. All human beings live in slavery if they do not live in accord with the *Pneuma*, the fiery immanent spirit within them. If they do not live in accord with their inner light of reason, they will be dominated within themselves and enslaved as a stranger to their true belonging.

If the community authoring the Gospel lived in Alexandria, in Egypt, or in cities such as Antioch or Damascus in Syria or Ephesus

Mummy Portrait of a Man, Egypt, Fayum region, site unknown, ca. 150–200 C.E., encaustic on wood, 17¾ x 10⅝ inches. Photography: Hickey & Robertson, Houston. Permission granted for reproduction courtesy of the Menil Collection, Houston.

in Asia Minor, their historical context in the early second century would have alternated between times of peace and stability and times of conflict. There would have been bitterness, and violence among groups of people of differing ethnicities, struggling to survive under Roman domination. Participation in the governance of the cities came through Roman citizenship but that was not ordinarily given to those who had been collected into the category of natives or barbarians, Jews, women or slaves. There would have been many inhabitants in the cities and in the countryside that were powerless to exert any kind of political or social influence.

We can only suppose that the community of the Gospel of Mary had found a freeing message. The stories that community had heard about Mary

Magdalene, Peter, Andrew, and Levi in conversation with Jesus about the Human One must have brought them strength and courage and stability and peace in their struggle for freedom as true human beings. The message of our human and divine interconnectedness and the spiritual steps to peace given in the Gospel would have provided an answer to their life situations. A spiritual path inward to our shared humanity and divinity, as taught by a master, could set one free, if not in circumstance, at least from within. This is what Roman Stoics had understood, and perhaps these Christians thought similarly. Freedom and peace would mean different things in different circumstances. It could mean spiritual peace and freedom or

Mummy Portrait of a Woman, Egypt, Fayum region, Er Rubayat, ca. 150–200 C.E., encaustic on wood, 15¾ x 8⅞ inches, 40 x 22.5 cm. Access # CA 7124. Photography: Hickey & Robertson, Houston. Permission granted for reproduction courtesy of the Menil Collection, Houston.

political and social peace and freedom, whether one were Hebraic or Greek, Roman or Egyptian, Syriac or Persian.

It is interesting that Stoicism was never condemned by Christian orthodoxy. It spread into the popular mind throughout the Hellenistic world and its thought patterns were felt among Christian writers. By the medieval period, however, its influence had gone underground and its liberating optimism had become largely unconscious.

We have learned to think of Syria as a place in the early centuries still receptive to the energies of the Great Mother. We know of a similar influence in Egypt with Isis as goddess of fertility and motherhood and in Asia Minor with the mother of all gods Kybele, later brought to Rome.[110] Mary's sacred knowledge may have been better understood in locales where the ancient Great Mother had first taken hold in religious thought and in regions where its nuances had not been completely suppressed. Perhaps it was not as difficult for peoples in these regions to consider women as wisdom figures filled with creative mystical fire.

After the fifth century, what happened to the Gospel according to Mary? Why did it not win out or flow into mainstream Christianity is a question worth asking. Is it fundamentally flawed or false as an interpretation of the teaching of Jesus, or is it a way to salvation known in the early years, then found later to be wanting by the powers that be, and so that by the fifth century its ray of light had been mostly put out?

16

—✿—

Magdalene Spirituality
Struggles and Celebrations

WHAT WE DIDN'T KNOW in embarking on the study of the Gospel of Mary was that it would call us into an ascent of our souls, one that does not come without struggle. Possibly we wouldn't have been willing to embark, had we known where the Magdalene mystique was taking us. We, too, like the soul in the Gospel of Mary, would have to deal with the powers that dominate our souls—a task not unlike the third task given to Psyche by Aphrodite: to collect clear water in a bowl to be brought back from the steep mountain peaks and craggy cliffs where dark waters flow, nourishing the swamps of the River Styx. Yet, all in all, we somehow have been gifted to take up the task, not unlike Psyche does in Lewis's version, where she is singing and in good heart, even as she comes to the foot of the precipices: for an eagle comes to her and takes her bowl and brings it back to her brimful of the water.[111]

It is the ascent of the soul section in the Gospel of Mary that occupies much of our study and conversations in the interfaith Rothko Chapel, where we began to meet in 2005 on Sundays. The soul in the Gospel of Mary has to work through its own darkness, its cravings, its ignorance, and wrath. Embedded in this Gospel section are powers that translate from the ancient Coptic into modern English as "lethal jealousy" or zeal for death, enslavement to the body, intoxicated and guileful wisdom. And interestingly, all the dominating powers in the Gospel of Mary are manifestations of wrath. These are powers so obviously not limited to an ancient age but powers crucial for us to grapple with today.

The Gospel of Mary teaches an inner path to spirituality and living in peace, justice, and mission. Mary Magdalene understands these teachings of Jesus. She has looked inward to the Human One within herself. She has struggled through seven steps in her soul and has developed equanimity and peace. Reunited with her root and her glory, she is loving and fearless and spiritually powerful. As Vera-Ellen in our community reminds us: "Her focus was on the interior and her resonance with the Divine—this was the way it was with Jesus all the time." This is the way it can be for us, in moments of resurrection here and now.

When we are separated from our roots in God, we are out of "harmony," according to the Gospel of Mary. That is why the Teacher says, "Be in harmony. If you are out of balance, take inspiration from manifestations of your true nature" (Leloup translation). How fresh this sounds to our ears! Becoming harmonious involves becoming conscious of our true nature and recognizing of our true rootedness in God. The process of coming into balance, into health, and into life, is a process of recognizing our own divine humanity within. We are made in the image of God, we mirror God, we result from God, we exist in God. Recognition of our true nature begins a movement into harmony and health. This is a different voice than that of Paul, who emphasizes our sinfulness, rather than our goodness; this is a different orientation where our true nature is the focus rather than our vulnerability to evil. In this Gospel we are called into an interior place of recognizing our own divine humanity within. This is an ongoing mystical practice.

We do this work of reuniting with God, for we carry the seed of the descending and ascending one within us. In more traditional terms, we carry the Christ within us. We may prefer to speak of the Human One or True Humanity as dwelling within us. When we connect deeply to the Human One within us, we connect deeply to our own descending character—that is, our original home of having been made in the image and likeness of God and implanted with the seed of unification in our walking faithfully and with loyalty to God.

After our year's study of the Gospel of Mary, we moved into another phase. We had noted the conversation-in-community that emerges from the Gospel's pages. We saw that its content placed us in conversation with other views—those of other Gospel writers in the early days of the Christian movement, with Jewish mystical views, with those of the Greco-Roman world, with goddess spiritualities. With its affinities with Buddhism and Taoist thought, the Gospel of Mary enters into dialogue with Eastern spiritualities as well. We had become interested in Islam and in the Baha'i Faith that looks to the "Most Great Peace" and the bonds of affection and unity between nations and peoples. For us, this openness to the connections between ways of thinking and believing was a big part of the Magdalene's appeal.

So we began to think of ourselves as a connective community seeking conversation with other spiritualities and religious traditions, and to come together regularly on the day of resurrection. We wanted to make connections, to resist divisions and separations, and to help break down barriers and boundaries that keep us divided from those of other faiths and persuasions. We wanted to step forward in connecting to all of the various spiritualities and religious traditions represented in Houston. We were welcomed and began convening our services at the interfaith chapel in Houston known as the Rothko Chapel.

Before you walk into the darkened space of the Rothko Chapel, you can pick up any number of books about Buddhism, copies of the Torah and the Qu'ran and the Holy Bible. Some of the faiths represented at the Rothko Chapel we know little about. We are beginners in interfaith dialogue. It is the desire for peace that persuades us of our mission.

As we enter the chapel space and move into the silence and stillness and darkness shrouded by the deep purple hues of the abstract paintings that cover the wall, we first sit in the darkness, before we begin to see the light. The light comes in the opening silence or in the music or dance or in the opening dialogue and the readings, or in the conversation. We are given insight from the meditation of our own hearts and from the gift of our true humanity from within. And we feel more connected to cultures and understandings that we've never studied before through the various readings that are offered. The notion of "stranger" seems farther and farther away from our lips. We feel we are developing into a truly connected humanity. Perhaps it is because we are moving more deeply into what seems like a strange part of ourselves—the mystical side of humanity that seems to be opening all around us in these post-rationalist times.

It was in the darkness, according to the Gospel of John, that Mary Magdalene made her way to the tomb on the first day of the week. At the tomb the light from the angels appeared to her in a vision and she heard the voice of her beloved calling her. It was a voice of empowerment and hoped-for consolation for the Magdalene. Jesus urged her to find her own path to God and to share his words with those he now calls his brothers. We are all sisters and brothers of the incomprehensible God of the many names. It is up to us to find our own way to the Light. The good news is that we can all share the peace of the incomprehensible Light.

Our first service of peace, harmony, and health was held, ironically, on September 11, 2005. We first observed silence after a meditation written for our space of Rothko paintings:

First we wrap ourselves in silence
In emptiness and nothingness
In no-thing-ness
We let go of the things of this world that press in on us, that call us.

We sink more deeply into ourselves in our rooted-ness
In our radicality—as rooted in the Good and the Just, in the Beautiful
 and in the Love.
We remain still in this space of silence.
We wrap ourselves in the canvas of purple and dark hues that we see
 before us.
In the comfort of the true humanity and divinity that resides within
 each of us.
No matter the way we look, or our differences,
 our age or the color of our skin, the gender we embody, the
 nationality or religious tradition out of which we live.
We are together here in community as true human beings.
And in the dark we await for the light.
We await to see.
We await for the silence to break into speech.
Mary Magdalene ventured boldly to the tomb while it was still dark.
She awaited for the light of angels and the prophetic seeing
 and speaking.
We follow her example.

Then our service progressed to Jesus' greeting to his disciples from the Gospel of Mary, a greeting that has become our community's tradition: "Peace be with you. Acquire my peace within yourselves" (King). We included the words of Jesus about the intertwining of all natural phenomenon: "All that is born, all that is created, all the elements of nature are interwoven and united with each other" (Leloup).

We went beyond the Christian tradition and read from Thich Nhat Hanh's *Peace is Every Step*:

 The roots of war are in the way we live our daily lives—the way
 we develop our industries, build up our society, and consume
 goods. We have to look deeply into the situation, and we will see
 the roots of war. We cannot just blame one side or the other. We
 have to transcend the tendency to take sides—that would be very
 helpful. We need links. We need communication. Practicing
 nonviolence is first of all to become nonviolence. Then when a
 difficult situation presents itself, we will react in a way that will

help the situation. This applies to problems of the family as well as to the problems of society.[112]

The Gospel of Mary and the study of the encounter of Jesus and Mary Magdalene in the garden have led us to a more mystical way of living, and our gatherings may work better with small communities than with large congregations. Ours is a more spontaneous and less fixed way of being together. Because our way is creative and visionary and mystical, it breaks out from the boundaries of a set liturgy and from formal rules and regulations. Our spirituality continues to be in process—it's never quite *here* and doesn't have as its goal to be *there*. We are quiet, connective, and conversational.

 Voices of the Magdalene Community

Just for a moment let me take you into this contemporary community to hear some of our voices talk about what they're looking for—and what they've found.

"What is it about the Magdalene that attracts you in the first place? Why did she draw you in? Is it Mary, or is it something else?"

"It's the message, more than the messenger—the message from the Teacher about the Human One. I think I am changing. The traditional Gospels seem more about proving a fact. The Gospel of Mary is more about love and mystery."

"It's the justice and the calm. When I hear the words 'Peace be with you. Acquire my Peace within you' I stretch out my arms in an enfolding gesture and I feel the peace."

"It's the interconnectedness of all things that gets me. I have been reading about that and here in the Gospel of

Voices continued…

Mary we find this idea—it's the first idea that surfaces in the Gospel—the disciples ask Jesus about matter—if matter will be utterly destroyed or not. Then they ask him about sin. What is sin? The answer to the first is that all the elements of nature are interwoven and united with each other. The answer to the second goes right through you, for the Teacher says there is no sin in any original sense, it's what we do to one another that generates the sin. That's not the message you get in the church!"

"It's the Magdalene herself that draws me in. She is very real for me. She was a person—not a symbol or representative. She was the authentic voice of Christ. That's why we come here—to hear what that voice is, without all of the church stuff. To me she is very real."

"But the church shut it down, but why?"

"That's a long and old story of divisions rather than connections."

"I love that her Gospel starts off with the question of matter—do we matter? It's a different take on that word, but what she has done for us is to say we do matter—that's part of that attraction for me."

"I think she was a historical person. I don't even want to start doubting that. Then I have no place to start."

"What she got was never going to pay for buildings and cathedrals and gold trimmed robes."

"What Jesus taught wasn't going to do that either."

"What they got was the original good."

"And it all comes from love—you don't need all these rules if you come from love."

Voices continued...

"I think that divinity is in all of us—when we explore other religions, we find that. We are always looking for a connection with a higher being, but it has to be somewhere in there to start the looking."

"I get so much out of these studies and then the conversation in our Sunday services. To me that's enough right now. I am on a path inward, so I can go out."

"To me it is so much more than what I've been getting I can't conceive of more. There may be more, but this is enough."

Perhaps we've found the Grail of True Humanness!

The Framework of Our Services

We have developed a general framework for our services. It is very simple, beginning with an opening greeting and dialogue, or with opening music or a quiet meditation. We alternate readings and silence or readings and music or dance. We think that music and movement or dance prepares us for the conversation as much as do the words of our readings.

In the middle of the service we have a "call to conversation" that is free-form and flowing. A leader facilitates the conversation. The conversation usually consumes thirty minutes of our time, after which we close with quiet meditation, music, or a closing dialogue. The general framework is as follows:

Opening Music

Call to Silence and Opening Meditation

Opening Greeting

Opening Dialogue

Readings and Meditation

Hymns or Music

Readings and Meditation

Call to Conversation

Closing Music

Closing Dialogue

Our contemporary gathering varies each time. On most Sundays, first there is silence and meditation, then music and dance serving as catalysts for conversation. In our readings of prayers and meditation, we move easily from the Hebrew Scriptures to the Christian Scriptures, drawing connections between the visionary and mystical experiences of Ezekiel and Daniel, and the visionary experience of Mary Magdalene in the garden on Easter morning. We read from the Wisdom literature that was alive to Jesus and Mary Magdalene in their day, and from the Hebrew prophets, especially the women prophets of early Judaism. We particularly enjoy beginning with this meditation by Rav Abraham Isaac Ha-Kohen Kook, Orot Ha-Kodesh:

> If you want, O creature of flesh and blood,
> Contemplate the light of God's presence
> throughout all creation.
> Contemplate the ecstasy of spiritual existence
> and how it suffuses every dimension of life . . .
> Meditate on the wonders of creation and the
> divine life within them.
> Know it as reality within which you live.
> Know yourself and know your world.
> Know the meditations of your own heart
> and of every sentient being.
> Locate the source of life deep within you,
> high above you, and all around you—
> The wondrous splendor of life within which you dwell.[113]

Vera-Ellen in our community has said of our services: "This is what the mystical body of Christ is. There is much spiritual power in this room. The power of sung word and spoken word that was surely present in early mystical communities. The energy is exploding in this magnificent chapel. It is palpable."

We move easily from the Christian canonical Scriptures to the extracanonical writings to discover more deeply how the Magdalene was remembered by her followers and to learn of her teaching and preaching. In our services, we select readings from the extracanonical materials that enter into dialogue with canonical readings, and with other readings from other spiritualities and religious traditions. As we sort through this amazing variety of writings, we come to know more deeply the divine—and ourselves.

One opening and closing dialogue we are fond of using is inspired by both the Gospel of Mary and the Gospel of Thomas:

Opening Greeting

Solo: Peace Be With You.

Unison: Acquire My Peace within you.

Opening Dialogue

Solo: Where are you from?

Unison: We have come from the place where light is produced from itself.

Solo: Where is that place?

Unison: It's a mystery.

Solo: But can you say you image the light?

Unison: Yes, indeed. We carry the light within.

Solo: And the peace?

Unison: Yes, also the peace.

Solo: How do you know of such light and such peace?

Unison: The sign is the feeling.

          The sign is the movement from within.

          The sign is the passion for the well-being of all.

Solo: What are your other signs?

Unison: Our recognitions of injustice and hatred and oppression
          throughout the globe, of power struggles and violence that
          seem unending.

Solo: Can we turn those around?

Unison: We must seek to do so.

Solo: Are you willing to spread your light and your peace?

Unison: We are eager to spread them.

          They spread just as love spreads.

Solo: The kingdom spreads out on the earth, just as love spreads.

Unison: But some people are not aware of it.

Solo: Yet you are aware.

Unison: Yes, indeed.

          We are aware of the light and the movement and the peace.

          And we cannot stand back.

          We will step forward.

          We will overcome the violence, the domination, the hatred,
          and spread love.

Closing Dialogue

Solo: Are you aware of the light and the peace within you?

Unison: We have the feeling and the movement,

          The passion for the well-being of all.

Solo: Light spreads, just as love spreads.

          Are you willing to speak your feeling of light?

Unison: Yes, indeed, we must speak the feeling.

          We must act the peace.

Solo: Let us move together

          In the light and the peace.

Unison: Let us go forth in the power of the Spirit.

In our contemporary Magdalene community we see in Mary's Gospel a wonderful optimism about human nature: an understanding of the goodness and true humanity of everyone as created in the image of God. In the Magdalene's story, our true humanity binds us to one another and makes us responsible to work for justice and peace in the world. Sometimes we begin our gatherings with this prayer:

Oh God, you have created us in your own Image and made us worthy to stand before you. We do not waver in your presence, but seek it, that through your grace we may deepen our sense of belonging to you. We pray your Spirit to fall upon us that we may be transformed into our true humanness, that we may know and feel, with the assuredness of Mary of Magdala and Levi, that you reside within us now, and forever. For yours is the power and the glory, the grace and the love that is everlasting. Amen.

As we gather together, we consider ways to stand with those unjustly treated, as the Magdalene stood by Jesus. We name our central concern a politics of reconciliation and peace, and we call the Gospel of Mary a Gospel of Peace. It is peace as political justice, when people pledge not to harm one another and to seek peace between warring nations. In this Gospel, Jesus is handing over to the disciples the oneness and peace he has known. He is saying, you too can know this peace. You too can experience union with the Light. You, too, can become transfigured in the peace.

"Peace be with you" isn't just a salutation with which we greet one another in the Magdalene community. It's our way of empowering one another, and ourselves, with the peace we seek to acquire in our spiritual journey—not a sentimental peace but a spiritual goal. It may be understood within the context of first-century Jewish mysticism. *Devekuth*, or "clinging to God," may be understood as similar to the Roman concept of *ataraxy*, or "equanimity."[114] We often recall Jesus' words to his disciples from the Gospel of Mary: "Peace be with you—may my Peace arise and be fulfilled within you. Be vigilant, and allow no one to mislead you by saying: 'Here it is!' or 'There it is!' For it is within you that the Son of Man dwells" (Leloup). Becoming the shared peace is a deeply interiorized spirituality. Yet it is a peace inviting questions and dialogue and conversation. It brings issues out into the open and moves against injustice nonviolently and proactively.[115]

One of our prayers disdains violence in any form:

O Divine Spirit of God, move us into perfect freedom. Save us from the entrapments of the world, its rivalries and hostilities, its cruelties and violence that sow discord and not harmony. Replace our judgments with compassion, our silence with speaking, our weeping with joy. Help us not to be deceived by the illusions of privilege that we carry. Teach us to eschew violence in any form.

> Transform us into true humanness that we may be a force for good
> and reconciliation and unity in the world. Amen.

In our ritual of the blessings of the waters, we give thanks for
the gift of water and its symbolic associations with blessing and
grace, wisdom and liberation in many spiritual traditions. For
centuries water and rivers and sacred wells have been associated
with personal transformation and healing, and with the recitation of
prayers and the performance of rituals. We add to these associations
a commitment to justice and the preservation of creation. We
repeat these words as a blessing:

> May there be peace in the world, where we join together, young
> and old, rich and poor, male and female, Semitic and European,
> black and white, gay and straight, and joined together may we
> open our hearts with love, seeking understanding of the truths of
> the sacred traditions—the truths of the Christian Scriptures,
> canonical and extracanonical, the truths of the Hebrew Scrip-
> tures, the truths of the Qu'ran, and of native peoples, and the
> truths of the sacred books and spiritualities of the East. Amen.

The more we read about Mary Magdalene, the more we find our
own spiritual experiences confirmed in hers. And the more we know
about Mary, the more we wonder: Is this community a simple detour
from the main path, or is it a point of contact with an ancestor who
can enrich our tradition today? How will the future of the Christian
tradition be changed if we recognize the marginal voices, the per-
ceptions and insights of women and others unjustly excluded across
the centuries? In the Magdalene of the extracanonical literature, we
find an open and questioning spirit, congenial and conversational in
tone, worthy of emulation today as we move toward greater understanding of the world's varieties of religious experiences.

Our contemporary community wants to become a sheltering
and reconciling place in the world, a place that works in love and
has concerns for those who are unjustly treated in the world, as did
Jesus, and as did the Magdalene. But this sheltering place starts with
each of us in our own spiritual work. This work is not only prayerful

and contemplative, but activist as well. If we don't try to make the world more just and peaceful and reconciling by *becoming* more just, peaceful, and reconciling ourselves, who will?

We are inspired by our musicians: Anita Kruse, pianist, composer, and vocalist, Jennifer Kenny, flutist, Sandy Stewart, singer/songwriter, and Sonja Bruzauskas, mezzo soprano. The music that accompanies our services can be found on the CD entitled *A Magdalene Mystique: Songs from Within* by Anita Kruse that is sold with this book. Mantras and songs such as Anita's "There's A Peace" and "Be Present" are gifts to us in our community. You may find this music helpful for private devotion or for use in your community.

Usually our conversations in the Rothko Chapel center on the readings and the selection from the Gospel of Mary. The seven steps of spirituality we find in the Gospel are often topics for conversation. That ignorance, for example, is a dominating power hovering over us is a brilliant insight for our time. We often shun and suppress new information in science and psychology for fear of what these new insights might do to our most cherished beliefs and traditions. New information may shake our foundations, to use the words of Paul Tillich. It's interesting that in the Gospel of Mary, when the soul is becoming more and more in touch with its light, it's able to respond to the powers that accuse it of wickedness as a strategy for keeping it in ignorance. The soul says to the power of ignorance: why do you judge me, since I have made no judgment?

The soul, or perhaps the Magdalene in this case, makes no judgments as she learns to live more deeply in the light. She does not play the blaming game. Leloup reminds us that the blamer is the *diabolos* (or "divider" in Greek).[116]

Everyone has different needs. Some find penitential services in the church very important in their spiritual lives. I, for one, admit a resistance to such services. I have spent much of life in self-blame and for me a penitential service is so familiar that I have grown to think I am rewinding old tapes when I should be moving on. For me to feed the self-blamer is counterproductive.

What if our attraction to the Magdalene has something to do with coming to a new consciousness about ourselves? What if her mystique has to do with a new awareness that we have stressed our sins for too long at the expense of our true humanity and divinity?

In our community we have voiced the concern that when we spend our energies in self-blame and in judging ourselves, it spreads out in blame and in judgment to others. There is a danger about what we do with self-blame and self-judgment. Life is complicated. Events happen. It is easy to blame ourselves as the cause of the event when if we were to expand our knowledge base to include more data, we might find that we are not to blame at all. When we want to blame the other person—look at what s/he did to me—it may well be that s/he was totally unconscious of the slight or insult—that s/he was thinking of something else and would not for the world hurt you.

What if we were to cease blaming ourselves, and others, we ask, and instead begin to observe the pattern of causes and effects that have led to this state of suffering? What if we were to look inside and find a unifier rather than a divider: a creative spirit that lives within us that is holy. What if we were to try to unite to the holy and the sacred within us, that spark of divinity, rather than to continue to activate the blamer? When that blamer has been silenced within us and has been extricated, we are free. The blamer is no longer fed.[117] This is just one example of a conversation that takes place at Rothko.

It is said that early pilgrims from the sixth to the seventeenth centuries journeyed to Mary Magdalene's house in Magdala and to the church that the Empress Helena in the fourth century built in her honor. In our contemporary Magdalene community, we're especially fond of reading a travel account from thirteenth-century pilgrims who proclaimed "the gospel of the Magdalene" there:

> Then we arrived in Magdala . . . the town of Mary Magdalene by the Sea of Gennesaret. We burst into tears and wept because we found a splendid church, completely intact, but being used as a stable. We then sang in this place and proclaimed the gospel of the Magdalene there.[118]

Today in our community we imaginatively travel to the first-century international trading town of Magdala by becoming more aware each day of our own multicultural setting. We need go only a few miles downstream from our city to one of the largest international seaports in the world. Our Gulf Coast city, founded by Jewish and Christian merchants and traders, has become home within the last three decades to thousands of Asian Buddhists and Hindus, and Muslims, Sikhs, Jains, Zoroastrians from all over the globe. Incorporating new Americans into our already established lifestyle is part of the spiritual work of our city.

It is not by saying, "Come be like us," but in genuinely engaging in spiritual conversation and dialogue with our new neighbors that the Magdalene community practices its mission. Those attending the Jade Buddha Temple in our city, for example, may be unaware of Mary Magdalene, but their huge statue of the Bodhisattva Kuan Yin, embodying loving kindness and compassion and peace, connects positively with the spiritual values of our community. It is the spiritual practice of dialogue with our international neighbors that interests us, the actual engagement with our neighbors of other religious traditions.

Our spirits desire, as well, dialogue with our own tradition: conversation, for example, about the rule defining Christian Scriptures at one time in history but now found to be restrictive in understanding the leadership of women in the early days of Christianity. Some rules of exclusion are obstacles in our relationships with others whom we are called to love as ourselves. In our community we wonder what Jesus means when he says in the Gospel of Mary, "Do not lay down any rule beyond what I determined for you . . . or else you might be dominated by it."

Puzzling over which rules in our own tradition have come to enslave us is part of the work of the Magdalene community, just as it was part of my work as I made my way to Rosamond's house. When I felt the power of the Spirit in our communion together, I ceased to be dominated by a rule and felt comfortable standing in "the between" of our two religions. I remembered the words of Jesus to the Magdalene in the garden: Your God is my God, your Father is my Father. In my release I thought of the washing away of separations among peoples and chanted the baptismal words: there is no longer Semitic or European, male or female, slave or free.

When I was visiting the Islamic Sufi center with Zari, I picked up the Qu'ran and held it. I was comfortable in the between and remembered the words of Jesus to the Magdalene and to the other disciples: find the descending and ascending Human One within you. Reunite yourself with your roots. Be in harmony and when you feel out of balance, take inspiration from your true nature. Peace be with you. Acquire my peace within you.

Bringing beauty back from the underworld was Psyche's last task assigned to her by the goddess of love. Perhaps the Magdalene, whom we have seen as a Psyche figure, can help bring beauty back to our world of catastrophic divisions and separations. Perhaps the Magdalene mystique is calling us to dig deeply into ourselves and find there the divine force that unifies rather than divides. When Psyche is on her way back from the netherworld, carrying her jar of beauty, she still needs to "see." She opens the jar of beauty and looks inside, taking some of the divine beauty for herself. Though there is much ado about her action, the truth is that she finally can see her own breathtakingly beautiful truly human and divine face.

Appendix A

Thecla

We know of the legendary adventures of Thecla from *The Acts of Paul and Thecla*, which was probably written in the second century by an author who revered her memory and sought to emulate her witness. Her story begins in Iconium, in Asia Minor, as she sits by the window of a house adjacent to the one in which Paul is preaching about abstinence and resurrection. Although Thecla had been engaged to marry a young man, after hearing Paul she refuses him. She has decided to follow Paul's message and remain a virgin.

Because of the pleadings of Thecla's mother and her fiancé, the governor first imprisons Paul for his disturbance. Then when Thecla secretly visits Paul in prison, and her visit by night is revealed, she is accused of impropriety and condemned to die on the burning pyre. But Thecla is miraculously saved when the rain puts out the fire, and she and Paul escape and venture into another city to continue their missionary work. But here again, Thecla is condemned by the governor and this time must be thrown to wild beasts.

When the day of the beasts arrives, Thecla throws herself into a pit of water to end it all. But in the process of this most assured death, she is miraculously saved and discovers that she has baptized herself!

Dying with Christ, in Paul's theology, is a baptism into new life. Eventually, Thecla is released after having fought with the beasts. She spends the rest of her days teaching and preaching the gospel.

In the fourth and fifth centuries, Thecla's piety and asceticism as a virgin were greatly revered, and she became a model of woman's piety not only in Asia Minor but in Syria and Egypt. Monasteries were dedicated to her and today we have traces of her memory through portraits and remembrances. See the following for more about Thecla:

Davis, Stephen J. *The Cult of Saint Thecla: A Tradition of Woman's Piety in Late Antiquity*. Oxford: Oxford University Press, 2001.

Johns, Scott Fitzgerald. *The Life and Miracles of Thekla*. Cambridge: Harvard University Press, 2006.

Psyche

The mythical tale of Psyche and Eros (Cupid) may have been part of popular lore in the ancient world, but the first time it is recorded is in the second century C.E. by Roman writer Apuleius (125–171) in his novel *Metamorphoses*. The tale has inspired many versions, including plays, poems, and novels, so to spin the tale as it has come down to us is an almost impossible task. For me, the mythical tale of Psyche—whose name means "soul"—is an allegory for the human soul that begins to discover its true self when it first discovers its own darkness. Out of this recognition, the soul works through the powers that dominate it, learning to rely on its own creative fire to discern the truth. As the soul progresses more deeply inward in its search for self, it can at last see its own truly beautiful face.

The tale as I am using it I briefly summarize:

Born the daughter of a king, Psyche is both breathtakingly beautiful and as natural as anyone could possibly be. But her gift of awesome beauty and vision condemn her to near death and destruction. The authorities in the kingdom—the king, the priests, and the people—decide that she's the sacrificial candidate they've been looking for: she can save the kingdom from all its woes, its famine and drought and plagues that have wasted it.

Psyche, who has innocently accepted her place in the universe as dictated by higher authority, is taken to a desolate place to meet her fate. She is rescued by the West Wind and taken to a splendid place where she lives with Eros, her god of love, in bliss but in darkness. Eros provides the love Psyche has been seeking, but he gives the command that she must live her nights with him in darkness. All seems well for a while, but there comes a time when Psyche needs to see, so she lights her lamp in the darkness to look upon the face of love.

Seeing what she wasn't supposed to see, she's abandoned and left on her own. Then her real story begins and she steadily and persistently, if painfully, goes more deeply into her own heart and finds resources she never knew she had. In the struggle, she creates new possibilities and in the end sees her own divinity. Aphrodite agrees to help Psyche if she can complete a seemingly impossible task: sorting a roomful of wheat, barley, beans, and lentils into tidy sacks— and finishing it all by twilight. And Psyche's struggles are far from over when she finishes tidying up the beans. Aphrodite gives three more jobs—going out into the sheep pastures and gathering an armload of their golden fleece, ascending to a steep mountain peak above a towering cliff to draw some clear water, and descending into the depths of the netherworld to bring beauty back in a jar. Psyche, grounded in the earth with the help of the natural creatures and her own natural self, successfully completes her tasks, as do those who have known her and loved her.

These tasks weave in and out of this book as a way of reminding the reader that the journey to the Magdalene is not merely of interest to a handful of people but is a journey far more mythical and universal than at first it might seem. The journey is to a more connected way of thinking and feeling that is emerging in our time. Psyche's development has to do with *our* development into a mode of being that is less oppositional and separating, more conversational and embracing, more connected and embodied. The new mode calls forth a new humanity that can contain more mystery, reflect upon new insights, and bring forth creative solutions to continuing problems. I owe much of my application of Psyche's tale to our journey to the Magdalene to Barbara Weir Huber, whose book, *Transforming Psyche*, brings together the tale of Psyche and models of human development. The version of the tale I rely on is the one told by C. S. Lewis in his last book, *Till We Have Faces*. Lewis retells Psyche's tale from the perspective of spiritual vision and also develops the character of Psyche's sister, Orual, as one of us. All of us, including Orual, have resonances with Psyche, as does the Magdalene.

Another Lost Thread: Origen (c. 185–c. 254) and Mary Magdalene

One peculiar feature of the Dura painting is that although the door to the tomb is open, the sarcophagus itself is not open, but closed. And a vine grows over it, as though the tomb has been in the chamber more than two days. Could it be that in this painting we do not have represented an "objective" event but a vision of the resurrection from the hearts and minds of these Christians? In my meditations on these paintings, I keep going back to Origen's sermon on Mary Magdalene where he speaks of the "tomb of our hearts." Other than the fact that Origen lived at the time these panels were painted, there is no historical reason that I know of to connect Origen's sermon with these lost paintings. Nevertheless, I include his words for their power and beauty about Mary Magdalene with the hope that they will further your meditation on this lost art, as they have mine. Origen's sermon is an elaborate discussion of the passage from John 20 where Mary Magdalene goes to the garden. He begins with her story that begins with line 11, and he praises her for her love for Jesus and her boldness of speech. He brings together the love between Mary Magdalene and Jesus with the Hebrew Song of Songs, which may more originally have belonged to Mesopotamian love poetry or wedding ritual. At the close of his sermon, Origen pleads with his listeners:

> Learn of Mary to seek for Jesus in the sepulcher of thy heart. Roll
> away the stone from the door of the sepulcher of God, remove all
> hardness, and put away everything that may hinder thy faith: take

away all worldly desire from thy heart, and search diligently whether Jesus be in it. And if thou find not Jesus in it, stand outside and weep . . . that he will vouchsafe to enter into thee and will dwell in thee . . . look often into the Sepulcher of God which is in thee . . . do not faint and give over, but weep and seek still Jesus in thy self, until thou find him. And if he by chance at any time to appear unto you and to present himself unto thy desire, do not presume of thyself as though thou knoweth him but inquire of him, and beseech him he will show himself unto thee. . . . So that thou will not need to ask of other, Where is Jesus, but thou wilt rather tell and show him to others. Say: for I have seen the Lorde, and he spoke these things unto me. To whom with the Father and the Holy Ghost be all honor and glory world without end. Amen.

Appendix B

THREE TRANSLATIONS OF THE COPTIC FRAGMENT OF THE GOSPEL OF MARY

Originally in Greek, the Coptic Copy, discovered in a Cairo marketplace in 1896, dates back to the fifth century and is known as Berlin Codex: BG 8502. (Pages 1–6 and 11–14 are missing)

Jean-Yves Leloup Page 7	Karen L. King [119]	Esther de Boer
[. . .] "What is matter? Will it last forever?"	"[. . .] Will m[a]tter then be utterly [destr]oyed or not?"	[. . .] Will [matter] then be [destroyed] or not?
The Teacher answered: "All that is born, all that is created, all the elements of nature are interwoven and united with each other.	The Savior replied, "Every nature, every modeled form, every creature, exists in and with each other.	The Saviour said, "All natural phenomena, all that has been moulded, all that has been brought into being exist in and with each other.

Jean-Yves Leloup Page 7 continued...	Karen L. King	Esther de Boer
All that is composed shall be decomposed; everything returns to its roots; matter returns to the origins of matter.	They will dissolve again into their own proper root. For the nature of matter is dissolved into what belongs to its nature.	And will be unloosened up again up to their own root, since the Nature of matter is unloosened up to what belongs to her Nature alone.
Those who have ears, let them hear."	Anyone with two ears able to hear should listen!"	He who has ears to hear, let him hear."
Peter said to him: "Since you have become the interpreter of the elements and the events of the world, tell us: What is the sin of the world?"	Then Peter said to him, "You have been explaining every topic to us; tell us one other thing, What is the sin of the world?"	Peter said to him, "Since you have told us everything, tell us this also: What is the sin of the world?"

Jean-Yves Leloup	Karen L. King	Esther de Boer
Page 7 continued...		
The Teacher answered: "There is no sin. It is you who make sin exist, when you act according to the habits of your corrupted nature; this is where sin lies.	The Savior replied, "There is no such thing as sin; rather you yourselves are what produces sin when you act in accordance with the nature of adultery, which is called 'sin.'	The Saviour said, "Sin does not exist, but you are the ones who sin when you do things which are like the nature of adultery: that is called sin."
This is why the Good has come into your midst. It acts together with the elements of your nature so as to reunite it with its roots."	For this reason, the Good came among you, pursuing (the good) which belongs to every nature. It will set it within its root."	Because of this the Good One came into your midst, to those who belong to all natural phenomena, in order to restore Nature up to her Root."
Then he continued: "This is why you become sick, and why you die: it is the result of your actions; what you do takes you further away.	Then he continued. He said, "This is why you get si[c]k and die: because [you love] what de[c]ei[ve]s you.	Then he continued and said, "That is why you become sick and die, for [. . .]

Jean-Yves Leloup	Karen L. King	Esther de Boer
Page 7 continued...		
Those who have ears, let them hear."	[Anyone who] thinks should consider (these matters)!"	[He who] understands, let him understand."
Page 8		
"Attachment to matter gives rise to passion against nature. Thus trouble arises in the whole body;	"[Ma]tter gav[e bi]rth to a passion which has no Image because it derives from what is contrary to nature.	"Matter [brought forth] passion that, since it proceeded from an opposite nature, has no form.
This is why I tell you 'Be in harmony . . .' If you are out of balance, take inspiration from manifestations of your true nature.	A disturbing confusion then occurred in the whole body. That is why I told you, 'Become content at heart, while also remaining discontent and disobedient; indeed become contented and agreeable (only) in the presence of that other Image of nature.'	From then on confusion exists in the whole body. That is why I said to you, 'Be fully assured and do not be persuaded (by what is opposite to Nature), since you are already persuaded (by the Good One) in the presence of the various forms of Nature.

Jean-Yves Leloup Page 8 continued...	Karen L. King	Esther de Boer
Those who have ears, let them hear."	Anyone with two ears capable of hearing should listen!"	He who has ears to hear, let him hear"
After saying this, the Blessed One greeted them all, saying: "Peace be with you—may my Peace arise and be fulfilled within you!	When the Blessed One had said these things, he greeted them all. "Peace be with you!" he said. "Acquire my peace within yourselves!	When the Blessed One had said this, he embraced them all, saying, "Peace be with you. My peace bring her forth to you.
Be vigilant, and allow no one to mislead you by saying: 'Here it is!' or 'There it is!' For it is within you that the Son of Man dwells.	Be on your guard so that no one deceives you by saying, 'Look over here!' or 'Look over there!' For the child of true humanity exists within you.	Beware that no one leads you astray, saying, 'Lo here!' or 'Lo there!' for the Son of Man is within you.
Go to him, for those who seek him, find him.	Follow it! Those who search for it will find it.	Follow him. Those who seek him will find him.

Jean-Yves Leloup	Karen L. King	Esther de Boer
Page 8 continued…		
Walk forth, and announce the gospel of the Kingdom."	Go then, preach[h] the good news about the Realm."	Go then and preach the gospel of the kingdom."
Page 9		
"Impose no law other than that which I have witnessed. Do not add more laws to those given in the Torah, lest you become bound by them."	"[Do] not lay down any rule beyond what I determined for you, nor promulgate law like the lawgiver, or else you might be dominated by it."	"Do not lay down any rule other than the one I appointed for you. And do not give a law like the lawgiver so that you are not imprisoned by it."
Having said all this, he departed.	After he had said these things, he departed from them. **GPO:** . . . having said [th]ese things, he de[parted.]	When he had said this, he departed.

Jean-Yves Leloup

Page 9 continued...

The disciples were in sorrow, shedding many tears, and saying: "How are we to go among the unbelievers and announce the gospel of the Son of Man? They did not spare his life, so why should they spare ours?"

Karen L. King

BG 8502: But they were distressed and wept greatly. "How are we going to go out to the rest of the world to announce the good news about the Realm of the child of true Humanity?" they said. "If they did not spare him, how will they spare us?"

GPO: [But they were distressed, weeping greatly.] "How [are we to] g[o to the rest of the world preaching the good] news of the Rea[lm of the child of true Humanity?" they said. "For if] they [did not spare him,] how will they keep [away from] us?"

Esther de Boer

But they were grieved and wept greatly, saying, "How shall we go to the nations and preach the gospel of the kingdom of the Son of Man? If they did not spare him, how will they spare us?"

Jean-Yves Leloup

Page 9 continued...

Then Mary arose, embraced them all, and began to speak to her brothers: "Do not remain in sorrow and doubt, for his Grace will guide you and comfort you. Instead, let us praise his greatness, for he has prepared us for this. He is calling upon us to become fully human [*Anthropos*]."

Karen L. King

BG 8502: Then Mary stood up. She greeted them all, addressing her brothers and sisters, "Do not weep and be distressed nor let your hearts be irresolute. For his grace will be with you all and will shelter you. Rather we should praise his greatness, for he has prepared us and made us true Human beings."

GPO: [Then Mary stood up and greeted] them; she tenderly kissed [them all and said, "Brothers and sisters, do not weep, do not be dis]tressed nor be in doubt. [For his grace will be w]ith you sheltering you. Rather [we should] praise his [greatn]ess, for he has united us and [made (us)] true Human beings."

Esther de Boer

Then Mary stood up, embraced them all, and said to her brothers (and sisters), "Do not weep and do not grieve and do not be in two minds, for his grace will be with you all and will shelter you. Rather let us praise his greatness, because he has prepared us. He has made us (true) Human Being."

Jean-Yves Leloup
Page 9 continued...

Thus Mary turned their hearts toward the Good, and they began to discuss the meaning of the Teacher's words.

Karen L. King

BG 8502: When Mary had said these things, she turned their heart [to]ward the Good, and they began to deba[t]e about the wor[d]s of the [Savior].

GPO: [When Ma]ry [said these things] she turned their mind to[ward the Good, and they began to deba[t]e about the sayings of the Savio[r].

Esther de Boer

When Mary had said this, she turned their hearts inward, to the Good One, and they began to discuss the words of the [Saviour].

Jean-Yves Leloup

Page 10

Peter said to Mary: "Sister, we know that the Teacher loved you differently from other women. Tell us whatever you remember of any words he told you which we have not yet heard."

Karen L. King

BG 8502: Peter said to Mary, "Sister, we know that the Savior loved you more than all other women. Tell us the words of the Savior that you remember, the things which you know that we don't because we haven't heard them."

GPO: [Peter said to] Mary, "Sister, we know that you were greatly [loved by the Sav]ior, as no other woman. Therefore tell us t[hose wor]ds of the Savior which [you know] but which we haven't heard." [Mary] re[plied, "I will] rep[ort to you as much as] I remember that is unknown to you." [And she began (to speak) the]se words [to them].

Esther de Boer

Peter said to Mary, "Sister, we know that the Saviour loved you more than the rest of women. Tell us the words of the Saviour which you remember, the things that you know and we do not, nor have we heard them."

Jean-Yves Leloup

Page 10 continued...

Mary said to them: "I will now speak to you of that which has not been given to you to hear. I had a vision of the Teacher, and I said to him: 'Lord I see you now in this vision.' And he answered: 'You are blessed, for the sight of me does not disturb you. There where is the nous, lies the treasure.'

Karen L. King

BG 8502: Mary responded, "I will teach you about what is hidden from you." And she began to speak these words to them. She said, "I saw the Lord in a vision and I said to him, 'Lord, I saw you today in a vision.' He answered me, 'How wonderful you are for not wavering at seeing me! For where the mind is, there is the treasure.'"

GPO: "When [the Lord] ap[peared] to m[e] in a vision, [I said], 'Lord, today [I saw y]ou.' He replied, ['How wonderful you are . . . '"]

Esther de Boer

Mary answered and said, "What is hidden from you I shall tell you." And she began to say to them these words: "I", she said, "I have seen the Lord in a vision and I said to him, 'Lord, I have seen you today in a vision.' He answered, he said to me, 'Blessed are you, because you are not wavering when you see me. For where the mind is, there is the treasure.'

Jean-Yves Leloup
Page 10 continued...

Then I said to him: 'Lord, when someone meets you in a Moment of vision, is it through the soul [psyche] that they see, or is it through the Spirit [*Pneuma*]?' The Teacher answered: 'It is neither through the soul nor the spirit, but the *nous* between the two which sees the vision, and it is this which [. . .]'"

Pages 11–14 are missing

Karen L. King

BG 8502: "I said to him, 'So now, Lord, does a person who sees a vision see it <with> the soul <or> with the spirit?' The Savior answered, 'A person does not see with the soul or with the spirit. Rather the mind, which exist between these two, sees the vision an[d] that is w[hat . . .]'"

Esther de Boer

I said to him, 'Lord, now, does he who sees the vision see it with the soul or with the spirit?' The Saviour answered, he said, 'He does not see with the soul nor with the spirit, but with the mind which [is] between the two that is [what] sees the vision and that [. . .]"

Jean-Yves Leloup

Page 15

"And Craving said: 'I did not see you descend, but now I see you rising. Why do you lie, since you belong to me?' The soul answered: 'I saw you, though you did not see me, nor recognize me, I was with you as with a garment, and you never felt me.' Having said this, the soul left, rejoicing greatly. Then it entered into the third climate, known as Ignorance. Ignorance inquired of the soul: 'Where are you going? You are dominated by wicked inclinations. Indeed, you lack discrimination, and

Karen L. King

BG 8502: "'. . . it.'" "And Desire said, 'I did not see you go down, yet now I see you go up. So why do you lie since you belong to me?' The soul answered, 'I saw you. You did not see me nor did you know me. You (mis)took the garment (I wore) for my (true) self. And you did not recognize me.' After it had said these things it left rejoicing greatly. Again, it came to the third Power, which is called 'Ignorance.' [It] examined the soul closely, saying, 'Where are you going?

Esther de Boer

him and Desire said "I did not see you, on your way downwards, but now I see you, on your way upwards. But how can you deceive me, when you belong to me?" The Soul answered and said "I have seen you. You did not see me nor recognise me. I was (like) a garment to you, and you did not know me." When she had said this, she went away rejoicing loudly. 'Again she came to the third Power which is called Ignorance. [She] questioned the Soul, saying, "Where are you going? In

Jean-Yves Leloup	Karen L. King	Esther de Boer
Page 15 continued…		
you are enslaved.' The soul answered: 'Why do you judge me, since I have made no judgment? I have been dominated, but I myself have not dominated. I have not been recognized, but I myself have recognized that all things which are composed shall be decomposed, on earth and in heaven.' Freed from this third climate, the soul continued its ascent, and found itself in the fourth climate. This has seven manifestations: the first manifestation is Darkness; the second, Craving;	You are bound by wickedness. Indeed you are bound! Do not judge! And the soul said, 'Why do you judge me, since I have not passed judgement? I have been bound, but I have not bound (anything). They did not recognize me but I have recognized that the universe is to be dissolved, both the things of earth and those of heaven.' When the soul had brought the third Power to naught, it went upward and saw the fourth Power. It had seven forms. The first form is darkness; the second is desire;	wickedness you were held prisoner. Yes, you were held prisoner. Do not judge then!" And the Soul said, "Why do you judge me when I do not judge you? I am taken prisoner although I did not take prisoners. I am not recognized, but I have recognized that the All is being unloosened, both the earthly and the heavenly things." When the Soul left the third Power powerless, she went upwards and saw the fourth Power. She took on seven appearances. The first appearance is Darkness, the second Desire,

Jean-Yves Leloup
Page 15 continued...

the third, Ignorance; the fourth, Lethal Jealousy; the fifth, Enslavement to the Body; the sixth, Intoxicated Wisdom; the seventh, Guileful Wisdom. These are the seven manifestations of Wrath and they oppressed the soul with questions: 'Where do you come from, murderer?' and 'Where are you going, vagabond?' The soul answered: 'That which has oppressed me has been slain; that which encircled me has vanished; my craving has faded, and I am freed from my ignorance.

Karen L. King

the third is ignorance; the fourth is zeal for death; the fifth is the realm of the flesh; the sixth is the foolish wisdom of the flesh; the seventh is the wisdom of the wrathful person. These are the seven Powers of Wrath. They interrogated the soul, 'Where are you coming from, human-killer, and where are you going, space-conqueror?' The soul replied, saying, 'What binds me has been slain, and what surrounds me has been destroyed and my desire has been brought to an end and ignorance has died.

Esther de Boer

the third Ignorance, the fourth is the Jealousy of Death, the fifth is the Kingdom of the Flesh, the sixth is the Foolish Learning of the Flesh, the seventh is the Hot Tempered Wisdom. These are the seven [power]s of Wrath. They ask the Soul, "Where do you come from, you killer of people?", or, "Where are you going, you who leave places powerless?" The Soul answered, she said, "What imprisons me is pierced. What turns me is left powerless and my Desire has been fulfilled, and Ignorance has died.

Jean-Yves Leloup

Page 15 continued...

I left the world with the aid of another world; a design was erased, by virtue of a higher design. Henceforth I travel toward Repose, where time rests in the Eternity of Time; I go now into Silence.'"
Having said all this, Mary became silent, for it was in silence that the Teacher spoke to her.

Karen L. King

In a [wor]ld, I was set loose from a world [an]d in a type, from a type which is above, and (from) the chain of forgetfulness which exists in time. From this hour on, for the time of the due season of the aeon, I will receive rest [i]n silence.'" After Mary had said these things, she was silent, since it was up to this point that the Savior had spoken to her.

PRyl: " . . . for the rest of the course of the [due] measure of the time of the aeon, I will rest i[n] silence.'" After she had said these [words], Mary was sile[n]t, for the Savior had spoken up to this point.

Esther de Boer

From a world I am unloosened through a world and from a model through a model which is from the side of Heaven. And the fetter of oblivion is temporal. From this hour on, at the time, of the decisive moment in the aeon, I shall receive the Rest in Silence." When Mary had said this, she fell silent, since it was to this point that the Saviour had spoken to her.

Jean-Yves Leloup

Page 15 continued...

Then Andrew began to speak, and said to his brothers: "Tell me, what do you think of these things she has been telling us? As for me, I do not believe that the Teacher would speak like this. These ideas are too different from those we have known."

Karen L. King

BG 8502: Andrew responded, addressing the brothers and sisters, "Say what you will about the things she has said, but I do not believe that the S[a]vior said these things, [for] indeed these teachings are strange ideas."

PRyl: Andrew sai[d, "B]rothers, what is your opinion of what was just said? Indeed I do not believe that the S[a]vior said these things, for what she said appears to give views that are [dif]ferent from h[is th]ought."

Esther de Boer

But Andrew answered and said to the brothers (and sisters), "Tell me, what do you say about what she has spoken? I at least do not believe that the Saviour said this. For these teachings seem to be according to another train of thought."

Jean-Yves Leloup
Page 15 continued...

And Peter added: "How is it possible that the Teacher talked in this manner with a woman about secrets of which we ourselves are ignorant? Must we change our customs, and listen to this woman? Did he really choose her, and prefer her to us?"

Karen L. King

BG 8502: Peter responded, bringing up similar concerns. He questioned them about the Savior: "Did he, then, speak with a woman in private without our knowing about it? Are we to turn around and listen to her? Did he choose her over us?"

PRyl: After examining these ma[tt]ers, <Peter said>, "Has the Sa[vior]spoken secretly to a wo[m]an and <not> openly so that [we] would all hear? [Surely] he did [not want to show] that [she] is more worthy than we are?" . . .

Esther de Boer

Peter answered and spoke about these same things, he reflected about the Saviour: "After all, he did not speak with a woman apart from us and not openly. Are we to turn and all listen to her? Has he chosen her above us?"

Jean-Yves Leloup	Karen L. King	Esther de Boer
Page 15 continued...		
Then Mary wept, and answered him: "My brother Peter, what can you be thinking? Do you believe that this is just my own imagination, that I invented this vision? Or do you believe that I would lie about our Teacher?"	**BG 8502:** Then [M]ary wept and said to Peter, "My brother Peter, what are you imagining? Do you think that I have thought up these things by myself in my heart or that I am telling lies about the Savior?" **PRyl:** " . . . about the Savior."	Then Mary wept, she said to Peter, "My brother Peter, what are you thinking? Do you suppose that I devised this, alone, in my heart, or that I am deceiving the Saviour?"
At this, Levi spoke up: "Peter, you have always been hot-tempered, and now we see you repudiating a woman, just as our adversaries do. Yet if the Teacher held her worthy, who are you to reject her? Surely the Teacher knew her very well, for he loved her more than us. Therefore let us atone, and become fully human	**BG 8502:** Levi answered, speaking to Peter, "Peter, you have always been a wrathful person. Now I see you contending against the woman like the Adversaries. For if the Savior made her worthy, who are you then for your part to reject her? Assuredly the Savior's knowledge of her is completely reliable. That is why he loved	Levi answered, he said to Peter, "Peter, you have always been hot-tempered. Now I see you arguing with the woman as these adversaries do. If the Saviour has made her worthy, who are you indeed to reject her? Surely, the Saviour knows her very well. This is why he loved her more than us. Rather let us be ashamed and clothe

Jean-Yves Leloup

Page 15 *continued...*

[*Anthropos*], so that the
Teacher can take root in us.
Let us grow as he demanded
of us, and walk forth to spread
the gospel, without trying to
lay down any rules and laws
other than those he witnessed."

Karen L. King

her more than us. Rather we
should be ashamed. We should
clothe ourselves with the perfect
Human, acquire it for ourselves
as he commanded us, and announce the good news, not laying
down any other rule or law that
differs from what the Savior said."

PRyl: Levi said to Peter, "Peter,
you are al[ways] rea[dy] to give
way to you[r] perpetual inclination
to anger. And even now you are
doing exactly that by questioning
the woman as though you're her
adversary. If the Savio[r] considered her to be worthy, who
are you to disregard her? For he
knew her completely (and) loved

Esther de Boer

ourselves with the perfect
Human Being. Let us bring him
forth to us, as he commanded
us. Let us preach the Gospel,
without laying down any other
rule or law than the one the
Saviour said."

Jean-Yves Leloup	Karen L. King	Esther de Boer
Page 15 continued...		
	her stea[d]fast[ly]. Rath[e]r [we] should be ashamed and, once we have clothed [ou]rselves with the p[erfec]t Human, we should do what [w]e were commanded. [We] should announce [the] good n[e]ws as [the] Savior sai[d], and not be la[y]ing down any rules or maki[n]g laws."	
	BG 8502: After [he had said these] things, they started going out [to] teach and to preach. [The Gos] pel according to Mary.	
When Levi had said these words, they all went forth to spread the gospel. *THE GOSPEL ACCORDING TO MARY*	**PRyl:** After he had said [the]se things, Le[vi] le[ft] (and) began to anno[unce the good ne]ws. [The Gospel according to Mary]	When [Levi had said] this, they began to go forth [to] proclaim and to preach. The Gospel according to Mary

Appendix C

The following are the core beliefs composed early in our development on retreat:

The Mary Magdalene Community is one of worship, celebration, and study. It is a connective community seeking conversation with other spiritualities and religious traditions.

The Community is part of the paradigm shift to a new world of reconciliation and understanding. Mary Magdalene is a liminal figure who calls us out. She is the threshold of the new paradigm.

We envision a Community that is a structure without walls. The Community is inclusive and open to all world religions, genders, faiths. The individual meets at the Group Consciousness.

Study is the cornerstone of the Community as we, individually and collectively, create our own tapestry of inclusiveness and understanding.

While we embrace the historical and scholarly study, we recognize that Mary Magdalene is the Mystical "something" that was left out.

We charge one another to recognize the evil that affects people from the start when they dwell with each other. We hold our core beliefs as the guiding principles in this process.

Women must be moved beyond the "Virgin" and "prostitute" image and become "certain" women. The women in the community speak as boldly as the men.

The Community moves beyond personal sensitivities and suffering.

We share the True Humanity/Divinity within us and it is the connecting link between us.

Each are connected forms of the sum of something greater.

The Community honors feelings and intuition, respecting the voice of each member and acknowledging the voice in our own being and our own voice of truth.

The Community embraces the concept of agreement and consensus versus majority.

Notes

Rosamond
1. See Appendix A for more about Thecla.

Finding an Ancestor to Bridge Separations
2. I have found the following helpful in understanding the contribution of St. Francis: Lawrence Cunningham, *Saint Francis of Assisi* (Boston: Twayne Publishers, 1976), 109–12; Roger D. Sorrell, *St. Francis of Assisi and Nature: Tradition and Innovation in Western Christian Attitude Toward the Environment* (New York: Oxford University Press, 1988), 142.
3. I will be calling upon three translations of the Coptic Gospel of Mary. This translation I owe to Karen King in her *The Gospel of Mary of Magdala: Jesus and the First Woman Apostle* (Santa Rosa, Calif.: Polebridge Press, 2003), 14. See Appendix B for translations.
4. Ibid., 18.
5. C. S. Lewis, *Till We Have Faces: A Myth Retold* (San Diego: Harcourt Brace & Company, 1957), 22, 102–5, 116.

Rediscovering Mary Magdalene
6. Susan Haskins, *Mary Magdalen: Myth and Metaphor* (New York: Riverhead Books, 1995).
7. See Appendix A for a fuller description of Psyche in both the older version of Apuleius and the newer version of C. S. Lewis.
8. Ann Graham Brock, *Mary Magdalene, The First Apostle: The Struggle for Authority* (Cambridge: Harvard University Press, 2003), 36–38. Brock cites the longer quote from Jane Schaberg.
9. It is generally agreed that verses Mark 16:9–20 were added to the original Gospel story in the second century. It may have been that the information about Mary Magdalene and demons was taken from the Gospel of Luke. For understanding Mark's story of Mary Magdalene, it is best to stop at verse 8.
10. de Boer, *The Gospel of Mary: Beyond a Gnostic and a Biblical Mary Magdalene*, (London: T&T Clark International, 2004), 164.
11. I have found this small book to be a useful handbook to the extracanonical literature: *The Gospels of Mary: The Secret Tradition of Mary Magdalene The Companion of Jesus*, edited by Marvin Meyer with Esther A. de Boer (San Francisco: Harper, 2004).

12. Brock, *First Apostle*, 83, citing Karen King, "Prophetic Power and Women's Authority: The Case of the Gospel of Mary (Magdalene)," in *Women Preachers and Prophets through Two Millennia of Christianity* (ed. Beverly Mayne Kienzle and Pamela J. Walker; Berkeley: University of California Press, 1998), 357–66.

Zari

13. Zari later gave me a book by the teacher Salaheddin Ali Nader Shah Angha entitled *Peace* (Verdugo City, Calif.: M.T.O. Shahmaghsoudi Publication, 1987). The website associated with the teacher is http://shahmaghsoudi.org.
14. Jane Schaberg, *The Resurrection of Mary Magdalene: Legends, Apocrypha, and the Christian Testament* (New York: Continuum, 2004), 300–356.
15. Salaheddin Ali Nader Shah Angha, *Peace*, 6, 20.

Images for a New Humanity in Dura-Europos

16. Lucinda Dirven, *The Palmyrenes of Dura-Europos* (Leide, the Netherlands: Brill, 1999), xvi–xvii.
17. Robin Margaret Jensen, *Understanding Early Christian Art* (London: Routledge, 2000), 62
18. Ibid.
19. Ibid.
20. Ibid., 37–39.
21. I am indebted to Susan Ashbrook Harvey and our correspondence for this historical perspective.
22. To cite two historians, Andre Grabar, *Christian Iconography: A Study and Its Origins* (Princeton, NJ: Princeton University Press, 1968), 20–21, and Jensen, *Early Christian Art*, 12.
23. Grabar, *Christian Iconography*, 21.
24. Carl H. Kraeling, *The Excavations at Dura-Europos Final Report VIII Part II, The Christian Building* (ed. C. Bradfond Welles; New Haven: Dura-Europos Publications, 1967), 80–81.
25. Grabar, *Christian Iconography*, 22.
26. Joseph Gutman, *The Dura-Europos Synagogue: A Re-evaluation (1932–1992)* (Atlanta: Scholars Press, 1992), 184–87.
27. Ibid., 166–67.
28. I am indebted to Susan Ashbrook Harvery for this point, again in our correspondence.
29. Kraeling, *Excavations*, 226.
30. Ibid., 213.
31. Ibid., quoting Jeanne Villette, 82.
32. Ibid., 80, 86.
33. Ibid., 78.
34. Ibid., 80.
35. Pasquale Accardo, *The Metamorphosis of Apuleius: Cupid and Psyche, Beauty and the Beast, King Kong* (Madison: Fairleigh Dickinson University Press, 2002), 109.

36. Gerasimos P. Pagoulator, *"Behold the Bridegroom": The Liturgy of the Bridal Chamber in Third Century Texts and in the Dura-Europos Christian House Chapel* (Dissertation presented to the Faculty of the Graduate School of Saint Louis University in Partial, 2000). Pagoulator studies the liturgy of the bridal chamber in the Gospel of Philip, the Acts of Thomas, and the *Symposium* by Methodius of Olympus in connection with the painting in the Christian building at Dura-Europos.

37. Ibid., 215–16. See also pages 210, 212.

38. Ibid., 229. See also 179, 225.

39. Buck, *Paradise and Paradigm*, 38.

40. See Appendix A for "Another Lost Thread: Origen and Mary Magdalene."

The Replacement of Mary Magdalene

41. A quote from Ambrose as found in Haskins, *Myth and Metaphor*, 90.

42. I am indebted to Harvey for this summary and her book with Sebastian Brock: Susan Ashbrook Harvey and Sebastian P. Brock, introduction and translation, *Holy Women of the Syrian Orient* (Berkeley: University of California Press, 1987).

43. Carmel McCarthy, *Saint Ephrem's Commentary on Tatian's Diatessaron: An English Translation of Chester Beatty* (Oxford: Oxford University Press on behalf of the University of Manchester, 1993), 331.

44. Ibid., 40.

45. Ibid., 68.

46. Ibid., 68.

47. Ibid., 96.

48. Again, I acknowledge my debt to Harvey in our correspondence.

49. Harvey and Brock, *Holy Women*, 8–9.

50. Robert Murray, *Symbols of Church and Kingdom: A Study in Early Syriac Tradition* (New York: Cambridge University Press, 1975), 329.

51. Deidre Good, *Mariam, the Magdalen, and the Mother* (Bloomington: Indiana University Press, 2005), Diane Apostolos-Cappadona, "On the Visual and the Vision: The Magdalene in Early Christian and Byzantine Art and Culture," 137.

52. Ibid., 135–36.

53. McCarthy, *Saint Ephram's Commentary*, 331.

Breaking Out of Old Stories: Sorting through the Commentaries and Legends in the West

54. Lewis, *Faces*, 299.

55. Carolyn Heilbrun, *Writing a Woman's Life* (New York: Ballantine Books, 1988), 42.

56. Lewis, *Faces*, 256.

57. Margaret Starbird, *Mary Magdalene, Bride in Exile* (Rochester, Vt.: Bear & Company, 2005), 11–12.

58. de Boer, *The Gospel of Mary*, 172–77.

59. Documentation for these historical positions and those that follow are found in King, *The Gospel of Mary of Magdala*, 149–150; Haskins, *Mary*

Magdalene, 91; and Katherine Ludwig Jansen, *The Making of the Magdalen: Preaching and Popular Devotion in the Later Middle Ages* (Princeton, N.J.: Princeton University Press, 2000), 54–55, Esther de Boer, *Mary Magdalen: Beyond the Myth* (Harrisburg, Pa.: Trinity Press, 1997), 6–64.

60. Schaberg, *The Resurrection*, 68.
61. Examples of the content of medieval preaching about Mary Magdalene have been brought together by Katherine Ludwig Jansen in *The Making of the Magdalen*, 149–150.
62. Ibid., 150.
63. Schaberg, *The Resurrection*, 80.
64. Jansen, *Making of the Magdalen*, 39.
65. Dan Brown, *The Da Vinci Code* (New York: Doubleday, 2003), 230–50.
66. Margaret Starbird, *The Woman With the Alabaster Jar: Mary Magdalene and the Holy Grail* (Rochester, Vt.: Bear & Company, 1993) and *Mary Magdalene, Bride in Exile*.
67. Starbird, *Bride*, 5.
68. Richard Leigh and Henry Lincoln, *Holy Blood, Holy Grail* (New York: Dell Publishing, 1982).
69. Lesa Bellevie, *The Complete Idiot's Guide to Mary Magdalene* (New York: Penguin, 2005).

Re-imagining Mary Magdalene as Jewish Visionary and Prophet

70. de Boer, *Mary Magdalene: Beyond the Myth*, 31.
71. Recently Bishop Spong in *The Sins of the Scripture: Exposing the Bible's Texts of Hate to Reveal the God of Love* (San Francisco: HarperSanFrancisco, 2005), 107, has suggested that there is no such place as Magdala on the grounds that no one has been able to locate it. Most scholars in Magdalene studies, de Boer, King, Schaberg, generally accept "Magdalene" to refer to her birthplace in Magdala.
72. I found this phrase in Martin Heidegger and have always remembered it. The phrase carries solidity about it that screams of the difficulty we have in getting out of our birth layers.
73. de Boer, *Mary Magdalene: Beyond the Myth*, 21.
74. Good, *Mariam*, 3–21.
75. The manuscript using "Mariam" that is quoted above is Codex Sinaiticus, the manuscript discovered in 1844 in the Convent of St. Catherine at the foot of Mount Sinai. The quotation is taken from Deirdre Good, "The Miriamic Secret," in *Mariam, the Magdalen, and the Mother*, 3–6.
76. Thinking oneself back to a particular time is the language used by Schaberg in *The Resurrection*.
77. Ibid., 55.
78. Jane Schaberg, *On the Cutting Edge* (New York: Continuum, 2004), 200.
79. Ibid., 199.
80. Ibid., 209.
81. Ibid., 203–5.
82. Ibid., 205.
83. Ibid., 209–10.

Re-imagining Mary Magdalene as Apostle of Love and Mystical Experience

84. Taking ourselves back to zero is the language of Beverly Lanzetta in her book on radical wisdom: Beverly Lanzetta, *Radical Wisdom: A Feminist Mystical Theology* (Minneapolis: Augsburg Press, 2005).

85. Quoted by Schaberg, *The Resurrection of Mary Magdalene*, 7, from an article by Elisabeth Schüssler Fiorenza entitled "Mary Magdalene, Apostle to the Apostles" *Union Theological Seminary Journal* (April 1975): 5–6.

86. Again, the use of the language of Martin Heidegger.

87. Lanzetta, *Radical Wisdom*, 7–26. Lanzetta speaks also of the "un-saying" of woman on the model of a meditative spirituality that employs negative theology to make progress toward its healing.

88. Neil Douglas-Klotz, *Prayers of the Cosmos: Meditations on the Aramaic Words of Jesus* (San Francisco: Harper, 1990), 2.

89. Violet, B. "Ein Versuch zu Joh 20 17," *ZNW* 24 (1925): 78–80.

90. Gershom Scholem, *Major Trends in Jewish Mysticism* (New York: Schocken Books, 1946), 96–97.

91. Starbird, *The Woman with the Alabaster Jar*. See introduction.

92. Jean-Yves Leloup, *The Gospel of Mary Magdalene* (Rochester, Vt.: Inner Traditions, 2002), 11.

93. de Boer, *The Gospel of Mary*, 157–58.

Seeing Is Believing

94. Leloup, *Gospel of Mary Magdalene*, vi–vii.

95. Ibid., 13–18. Leloup cites Henry Corbin, *The Voyage and the Messenger* (Berkeley: North Atlantic Books, 1998), 117–34. Corbin points out the importance of visionary knowledge in Islamic spirituality. Islamic visionary literature is extensive in Arabic and in Persian.

Gathering the Golden Fleece from Medieval Mystics

96. Lewis, *Faces*, 284.

97. Marguerite Porete, *The Mirror of Simple Souls* (New York: Paulist Press, 1979), 150.

98. Theresa of Avila, *The Interior Castle* (Mahwah, NJ: Paulist Press, 1979). I will be quoting from Theresa extensively in this chapter and I draw my reader's attention to the following pages for my quotations: 144–45, 35, 39, 37, 37, 172–94.

Other Old Stories

99. Daniel Boyarin, *Dying For God: Martyrdom and The Making of Christianity and Judaism* (Stanford: Stanford University Press, 1999).

100. Ibid., Boyarin, citing Philip S. Alexander, 7.

101. Ibid., 142.

102. Karen L. King, *What is Gnosticism?* (Cambridge: The Belknap Press of Harvard University Press, 2003) and *The Gospel of Mary of Magdala*.

Traces of a Lost Christianity in the Gospel of Mary

103. See the brief description given in this book on pages 75–76, or Schaberg's article found in *On the Cutting Edge*, 193–220.

104. de Boer gives the first translation in her *Mary Magdalene:Beyond the Myth* and the latter in *The Gospel of Mary*. I have brought together three translations of the Coptic from scholars and have placed them in Appendix B. I am grateful to the translators for authorization to use their translations. It is my hope that the chart will be of help to you in your own meditations. The three translators bring out various nuances that are possible in the translation. Together they seem more of a symphony of voices, a presentation of how we might blend our different perspectives when we read sacred Scriptures. In the future, rather than footnoting a specific translation, I will place the name of the translator in parenthesis following the quote.

105. See King, *The Gospel of Mary of Magdala*, 7–12, for a detailed description of the discoveries of the manuscripts.

106. de Boer, *Mary Magdalene:Beyond the Myth*, 79–80.

107. de Boer, *The Gospel of Mary*, 14.

108. de Boer, *Mary Magdalene: Beyond the Myth*, 120. In her forthcoming *The Mary Magdalene Sourcebook*, de Boer has translated parts of the fourth-century Acts of Philip, which present Mary as an apostle teaching and baptizing and being martyred in Hierapolis in Asia Minor.

109. E. Vernon Arnold, *Roman Soicism* (London: Routledge and Kegan Paul, 1958), 279.

110. For the goddess Kybele see de Boer, *The Mary Magdalene Sourcebook*, chapter 5 on the Acts of Philip.

Magdalene Spirituality

111. Lewis, *Faces*, 300.

112. Thich Nhat Hanh, *Peace Is Every Step: The Path of Mindfulness in Everyday Life* (New York: Bantam Books, 1991), 115.

113. Meditation by Rav Abraham Isaac Ha-Kohen Kook, Orot Ha-Kodesh "The Lights of Holiness," as quoted by Lawrence Kushner, *The Way into Jewish Mystical Tradition* (Woodstock, Vt.: Jewish Lights Publishing, 2001), 15–16.

114. Scholem, *Major Trends*, 96.

115. We have learned much of our understanding of nonviolence from Walter Wink, *The Powers That Be: Theology for a New Millennium* (New York: Doubleday, 1998), 121–22, and *Engaging the Powers: Discernment and Resistance in a World of Domination* (Minneapolis: Fortress Press, 1992).

116. Leloup, *The Gospel of Mary Magdalene*, 57, 101.

117. Ibid., 56–59.

118. Quoted from de Boer, *Mary Magdalene: Beyond the Myth*, 22.

Appendix B

119. Also included are translations from Parallel Greek Papyrus Oxyrhynchus 3525 (GPO), copy found in Egypt and published in 1983, dating to the third century; and Papyrus Rylands 463 (PRyl), Greek copy discovered in Egypt in 1917, dating back to the third century.

Bibliography

Accardo, Pasquale. *The Metamorphosis of Apuleius: Cupid and Psyche, Beauty and the Beast, King Kong.* Madison: Fairleigh Dickinson University Press, 2002.

Arnold, E. Vernon. *Roman Stoicism.* London: Routledge and Kegan Paul, 1958.

Bellevie, Lesa. *The Complete Idiot's Guide to Mary Magdalene.* New York: Penguin, 2005.

Boyarin, Daniel. *Dying For God: Martyrdom and The Making of Christianity and Judaism.* Stanford: Stanford University Press, 1999.

Brock, Ann Graham. *Mary Magdalene, The First Apostle: The Struggle for Authority.* Cambridge: Harvard University Press, 2003.

Brown, Dan. *The Da Vinci Code.* New York: Doubleday, 2003.

Brown, Raymond E. *The Gospel According to John.* Garden City, N.Y.: Doubleday, 1966.

Buck, Christopher. *Paradise and Paradigm: Key Symbols in Persian Christianity and the Baha'i Faith.* New York: State University of New York Press, 1999.

Burns, Rita J. *Has The Lord Indeed Spoken Only Through Moses?: A Study of the Biblical Portrait of Miriam.* Atlanta: Scholars Press, 1988.

Camp, Claudia. *Wise, Strange and Holy: The Strange Woman and the Making of the Bible.* Sheffield, England: Sheffield Academic Press, 2000.

Cunningham, Lawrence. *Saint Francis of Assisi.* Boston: Twayne Publishers, 1976.

de Boer, Esther. *Mary Magdalene: Beyond the Myth.* Harrisburg, Pa.: Trinity Press International, 1997.

———. *The Gospel of Mary: Beyond a Gnostic and a Biblical Mary Magdalene.* London: T&T Clark International, 2004.

———. *The Mary Magdalene Sourcebook.* London, New York: Continuum International. Forthcoming in 2007 (published in Dutch, May 2006).

Dirven, Lucinda. *The Palmyrenes of Dura-Europos.* Leide, the Netherlands: Brill 1999).

Douglas-Klotz, Neil. *Prayers of the Cosmos: Meditations on the Aramaic Words of Jesus.* San Francisco: Harper, 1990.

Fiorenza, Elisabeth Schüssler. "Mary Magdalene, Apostle to the Apostles," *Union Theological Seminary Journal* (April 1975): 56.

Gibbons, Dorothy. "Two Sides of the Same Path" in *Change* (December 2005), publisher@changemagazine.net.

Good, Deirdre. *Mariam, the Magdalen, and the Mother*. Bloomington: Indiana University Press, 2005.

Grabar, Andre. *Christian Iconography: A Study and Its Origins*. Princeton, N.J.: Princeton University Press, 1968.

Gutman, Joseph. *The Dura-Europos Synagogue: A Re-evaluation (1932–1992)*. Atlanta: Scholars Press, 1992.

Guy, Laurie. *Introducing Early Christianity: A Topical Survey of Its Life, Beliefs, and Practices*. Downers Grove, IL: InterVarsity Press, 2004.

Haskins, Susan. *Mary Magdalen: Myth and Metaphor*. New York: Riverhead Books, 1995.

Heilbrun, Carolyn. *Writing a Woman's Life*. New York: Ballantine Books, 1988.

Jansen, Katherine Ludwig. *The Making of the Magdalen: Preaching and Popular Devotion in the Later Middle Ages*. Princeton, N.J.: Princeton University Press, 2000.

Jensen, Robin Margaret. *Understanding Early Christian Art*. London: Routledge, 2000.

King, Karen L. *The Gospel of Mary of Magdala: Jesus and the First Woman Apostle*. Santa Rosa, Calif.: Polebridge Press, 2003.

———. *What is Gnosticism?* Cambridge: The Belknap Press of Harvard University Press, 2003.

Kraeling, Carl H. *The Excavations at Dura-Europos Final Report VIII Part II, The Christian Building*. (Edited by C. Bradfond Welles. New Haven: Dura-Europos Publications, 1967).

Lanzetta, Beverly. *Radical Wisdom: A Feminist Mystical Theology*. Minneapolis: Augsburg Press, 2005.

Leloup, Jean-Yves. *The Gospel of Mary Magdalene*. Rochester, Vt.: Inner Traditions, 2002.

Leigh, Richard, and Henry Lincoln. *Holy Blood, Holy Grail*. New York: Dell Publishing, 1982.

Lewis, C. S. *Till We Have Faces: A Myth Retold*. San Diego: Harcourt Brace & Company, 1957.

Lexicon Iconographicum Mythologiae Classicae. Zurich: Artemis Verlag, 1981–1999.

McCarthy, Carmel. *Saint Ephrem's Commentary in Tatian's Diastessaron: An English Translation of Chester Beatty*. Oxford: Oxford University Press on behalf of the University of Manchester, 1993.

Madigan, Shawn, C.S.J., ed. *Mystics, Visionaries, and Prophets: A Historical Anthology of Women's Spiritual Writings*. Minneapolis: Fortress Press, 1998.

Meyer, Marvin with Esther A. de Boer, eds. *The Gospels of Mary: The Secret Tradition of Mary Magdalene The Companion of Jesus*. San Francisco: Harper, 2004.

Murray, Robert. *Symbols of Church and Kingdom: A Study in Early Syriac Tradition*. New York: Cambridge University Press, 1975.

Newell, J. Philip. *The Book of Creation: An Introduction to Celtic Spirituality*. New York: Paulist Press, 1999.

Origen. *An homilie of Mary Magdalene: declaring her ferue[n]t loue and zele towards Christ*. London: Reginalde Wolfe, 1565. Microfilm. Ann Arbor, MI: University Microfilms International, 1984.

Pagoulator, Gerasimos P. *"Behold the Bridegroom": The Liturgy of the Bridal Chamber in Third Century Texts and in the Dura-Europos Christian House Chapel*. (Dissertation presented to the Faculty of the Graduate School of Saint Louis University in Partial, 2000.

Porete, Marguerite. *The Mirror of Simple Souls*. New York: Paulist Press, 1979.

Salaheddin Ali Nader Shah Angha. *Peace*. Verdugo City, Calif.: M.T.O. Shahmaghsoudi Publication, 1987. The website associated with the teacher is http://shahmaghsoudi.org.

Schaberg, Jane. *On The Cutting Edge: The Study of Women in Biblical Worlds*. New York: Continuum, 2004.

———. *The Resurrection of Mary Magdalene: Legends, Apocrypha, and the Christian Testament*. New York: Continuum, 2002.

Scholem, Gershom. *Major Trends in Jewish Mysticism*. New York: Schocken Books, 1946.

Sorrell, Roger D. *St. Francis of Assisi and Nature: Tradition and Innovation in Western Christian Attitude Toward the Environment*. New York: Oxford University Press, 1988.

Spong, Bishop. *The Sins of the Scripture: Exposing the Bible's Texts of Hate to Reveal the God of Love*. San Francisco: HarperSanFrancisco, 2005.

Starbird, Margaret. *Mary Magdalene, Bride in Exile*. Rochester, Vt.: Bear & Company, 2005.

———. *The Woman With the Alabaster Jar: Mary Magdalene and the Holy Grail*. Rochester, Vt.: Bear & Company, 1993.

Theresa of Avila. *The Interior Castle*. Mahwah, N.J.: Paulist Press, 1979.

Violet, B. "Ein Versuch zu Joh 20 17." *ZNW* 24 (1925), 7880.

Wink, Walter. *Engaging the Powers: Discernment and Resistance in a World of Domination*. Minneapolis: Fortress Press, 1992.

———. *The Powers That Be: Theology for a New Millennium*. New York: Doubleday, 1998.